SEEDS *for* HARVEST

KINGDOM BUILDING FOR CHRIST

A Ready Reference Guide for Church Planting

A STEP BY STEP PROCESS FOR PLANTING AND GROWING NEW CHURCHES

DR. GEORGE A. MILLER

Copyright © 2022 Dr. George A. Miller.

All rights reserved. No part of this book may be reproduced, stored, or transmitted by any means—whether auditory, graphic, mechanical, or electronic—without written permission of both publisher and author, except in the case of brief excerpts used in critical articles and reviews. Unauthorized reproduction of any part of this work is illegal and is punishable by law.

ISBN: 979-8-88640-649-8 (sc)
ISBN: 979-8-88640-650-4 (hc)
ISBN: 979-8-88640-651-1 (e)

Because of the dynamic nature of the Internet, any web addresses or links contained in this book may have changed since publication and may no longer be valid. The views expressed in this work are solely those of the author and do not necessarily reflect the views of the publisher, and the publisher hereby disclaims any responsibility for them.

One Galleria Blvd., Suite 1900, Metairie, LA 70001
1-888-421-2397

CONTENTS

Acknowledgement v
Dedication vii
Author's Note ix
Introduction xv

Chapter 1   Vision Focus and Strategic Planning 1
Chapter 2   Defining and Targeting Demographic Populations 13
Chapter 3   Recruiting a Church Planting Team 21
Chapter 4   Begin With an End in Mind: Identifying Resources 30
Chapter 5   Launch Publicly Your Vision with a Committed
            Core Group 39
Chapter 6   Mobilize and Evangelize the Un-Churched 46
Chapter 7   Strategies for Growing and Sustaining a New
            Church Plant 55
Chapter 8   Equipping Pastoral Leaders for Church Planting 81

Summary and Conclusion 99
Copyright Acknowledgements 103

ACKNOWLEDGEMENT

I acknowledge church planters everywhere for having the zeal to involve themselves in Kingdom Building. I acknowledge family members who will play a crucial role in supporting God's plan to carry out "The Great Commission". I also acknowledge our church planting team who was instrumental in the establishment of our new church plant.

Church Plant Team

Equilla Miller
Minister Alonzo Miller
Peggy Miller
Deacon Lee O. Mays
Elaine Mays
Troy Dempsey
Patricia Dempsey
Dorothy Triplett
Lavon Glen
Katherine Jones
Cutina Haynes

Delaphine Mays
Elder Larry Whitfield
Erica Jones
David Brent
Felecia Mays
Patricia White
Bobby J. White
Regina K. White
Regina K. White
Kimberly Haynes
Marvin White

DEDICATION

I dedicate this book with appreciation to my son and daughter in law, Elder Anthony and Krista Miller. They have been a great gift to the body of Christ in answering God's call upon their lives.

AUTHOR'S NOTE

"Seeds for Harvest" is written to aid prospective church developers in spiritual focus and direction as it relate to church planting. The ready reference guide offers step by step directions in the area of planning, organizing, net working, recruitment, church growth, and the establishment of a successful new church start.

The need for spiritual evangelism is at an all time high. The Body of Christ must engage themselves in mobilizing and expanding the Kingdom of God. Just as the human body must generate and replenish cells in the body to sustain life; the church should reach out to lost individuals for the purpose of carrying out God's plan of healing and restoration to a lost world. In order for a local congregation or religious organizations to survive they must thrive. The church planting process becomes crucial to the spiritual and financial longevity of any religious organization.

While church planting is a noble venture and a great spiritual calling, there are many challenges that will be encountered as the church planter endeavor to carry out God's plan. Those who feel the call of God to be church planters must be focused on the plan of God, just as football coaches have a game plan for every game. Coaches start with a game plan and prepare their players to carry out the scripted game strategy. The game plan must be followed and we must depend of God to give us the commitment and resolve to see it through. The game plan helps team members stay focused on what they know will work if they just stay with it. It keeps them from overreacting and allowing the fans to dictate to the team. Church planters should have a similar strategy to stay with the game plan.

Statistical data supports the fact that new church starts are needed in our communities. There is also research that supports the fact that it is much easier for individuals to join a new church plant than it is to become a member of an existing church. We also know from research that there are an enormous number of people who don't know Christ. Up to 40 % of the American population remains un-churched. The Bible clearly states that every human being matters greatly to God. God calls us to go and find the ones we can reach and walk with them long enough so they can introduce Christ to others. We also know that in fishing; the initiative is with the fisherman, not the fish!

The purpose for entering into church planting is driven by the Great Commission and a passion for the Gospel that invites people into a relationship with Jesus Christ and others who know him (Matthew 28:18-20). Church planting is a process by which new churches are established. This is usually accomplished with help from a denomination, a church planting center, a local church or churches, a network, an association, and sometimes individuals who work to carry out the vision God has given them. The term can be applied to the establishing of churches as a legal entity and organization, as well as establishing an organic simple church or house church.

Church planting may also be defined as initiating reproductive fellowships who reflect the kingdom of God in the world. Another similar term, the Church Planting Movement is defined as a rapid and multiplicative increase of indigenous churches planting churches within a given people group or population segment.

The experience of church planting can be potentially harmful for the planter and his family spiritually and morally. The time and pressure of ministry can take a toll on church planters and a good, safe, and humble accountability plan is essential to walking in integrity and honoring God. A leadership paradigm with an elder or experienced church planter can be of great value to those who become overwhelmed with the challenges of church planting ministry. I encourage church planters to find elders from a sending church or other church planters to help you out in this way. Accountability protects you from being disqualified in the process. Having a safe place to be held accountable is protection for your soul. It's like holding a shield out in front of your character. If you confess struggles and sin then you will be protected and restored. If you fail morally you will be removed and restored. Build a culture of confession and restoration for you and your church plant team.

It is also imperative to utilize strategic planning principles to avoid the error that church developers make of failing to see the importance of a permanent worship location. Churches used to be able to plant in a school and spend the first few years growing to a size where they could build their first building. Due to demographics and economics, I believe that our strategies should change with the times. In most cities you can no longer rent high school auditoriums so the only space available are elementary or junior high school cafeterias. This space only holds around 100-150 people and provides little to no space for children. Instead of planning on growing your church to 400-500 and then building, church planters should find an intermediate location to get to that goal. This could be six or seven thousand square feet of office space or storefront that used to be retail facility. You don't have to own it or build it, but you need to get serious about finding a location where people can come to you every week and know you are going to be there. Most churches double in size the weekend they move from being mobile to a more permanent building.

People are also less prone to give faithfully to a church that's mobile. They don't know if it will be there in two months so why sacrifice? But with a permanent location you are trying to reach supporters.

Just as the challenge of pasturing can be difficult for pastors; so is the challenge for church planters who will certainly face the difficulty of experiencing loneliness. I speak from experience and have been challenged by the church planting process. Unless you go into the church planting process ready it can really be an issue. Recent statistics show that up to 70percent of pastors regularly fight depression. 808 pastors were asked about the quality of their marriage and 77 percent of them said their marriage was "not good." I believe most of these issues would be reduced if pastors lived in the biblical community and depend on other Saints within that community. What many pastors don't realize is the social toll this new life will take on them and their families. Most Pastors work alone, and this is especially true for church planters.

A church planter is in denial that believes he does not need the community his members need. Our enemy, the Devil, loves it when church planters/pastors isolate themselves. We become easy prey when we try to stand alone. Our wives and children become easy prey when we try to make them stand alone. There is such an important need to build a strong community for the family. I believe family health and relationship stability should be a strong factor considered when seeking a church developer of planter to carry out the work of planting a new church start.

When new church plant ideas are developed, the question always comes; why do we need to start new churches when we have so many already? This is a question often posed to church planters by other Christians. Somehow the thought of a new church in their community seems to be a threat to those Christians whose churches are struggling to survive. It's also a relevant question for the Pastor who has a burden to expand the Kingdom of God. The simple answer is that the planting of new churches stands head and shoulders above every other strategy for reaching new people for Christ.

In spite of the numerous churches in our communities 70% of all Americans have no meaningful church relationship. Recent statistics show that there are 195 million un-churched people in America. This is ample evidence that there is plenty of fruit left in the harvest for all to have a bountiful crop. In light of the scope of the task we face to fulfill the Great Commission in our communities we should strongly consider the most effective means to get the job done.

One reason that more churches don't consider this an option is the irrational fear that their church will suffer in the process either through competition for members or diluted resources. These fears reveal a root of unbelief in the one who would be stalemated by them. Not only will the Gospel be advanced in the lives of new believers, the local church prospers as well. Church planting energizes the planting church by releasing new opportunities for ministry to develop. In addition it demonstrates positive forward movement to the congregation. Success in any area of ministry breeds success. It's contagious, and is very much needed!

The first question that comes to mind is where will the new pastors come from? They are among us. God's first law of creation is that everything reproduces after its own kind. Monkeys reproduce monkeys, sheep reproduce sheep, and pastors reproduce pastors.

Paul told Timothy, *"the things you have heard me say . . . entrust to reliable men, who will be qualified to teach others."* That simple statement describes 4 generations of leaders who are advancing the Kingdom in the lives of others. The key is to develop the reliable leaders in our midst by entrusting ministry to them. Once a responsibility is entrusted you soon find out who is reliable and who is not. Those that are faithful entrust more and more into their care until they are ready to launch.

It is very needful and necessary that funds are set aside to invest in the process of church planting. When the vision is given from God the church planting process can proceed on schedule. When a new church is planted sending congregations should liberally contributes to the process and it is amazing how quickly the resources grow. I am thankful to see God bless our efforts to sustain a new church start. With the help of God all things are possible.

It is imperative that a doctrinal and philosophical position need to be established in the beginning of the church plant efforts. The church planter needs to be intentional in defining the new plant position early because the doctrinal position will be tested. Determine which theological issues you will fight for or willing to loose people over. The doctrinal position needs to be decided early and needs to be written down. If you are part of an organized body share your mission statement and the position that your church take. If you are a new church start you want to avoid the experience of having people come in and stand against the church plant position. Develop your statement of faith and teach your position. When the new church plant takes a stand on paper, there is minimal argument, only teaching and guiding. Use a good, biblical, well thought out "Statement of Faith" to ward off wolves and false teachers. I pray that God will grant the vision and zeal to see His work through.

Elder George A. Miller, Th. D

INTRODUCTION

Many times during my twenty six year tenure as a pastor, I wondered what it would be like to start a new church. Many times the Spirit of God challenged me to launch out in the deep and take a faith walk. As the years continued to pass, a still quiet voice continued to draw me closer to the vision and will God had for my life.

Eventually the opportunity came to be used by God in a mighty way. While considering the challenge of church planting and walking in faith, much prayer and fasting had to be done. I learned many lessons as I followed the leading of God to expand His Kingdom. I learned that successful church planting requires an undying commitment to the Lordship of Jesus Christ. It also requires a commitment to telling your vision over and over again . . . to neighbors, to friends, church leaders and to partner churches. It required soul searching, pavement pounding, door knocking, financial surrender, personal confession, ceaseless praying, vision casting, initiative, drive, heart, guts, passion, sweat, blood, and tears. It takes long hours and it takes hard work!

In establishing and developing a new church plant, the church planter will wear many hats; the hats may include accountant, secretary, worship leader, carpenter, nursery worker, sound man, painter, plumber, graphic designer, drummer, Sunday school teacher, greeter, coach, janitor, doorman, marketing coordinator, and so much more. The difficulty of the process is challenging but the joy that I found in the work of the Kingdom far exceeded any difficulties that were experienced. Church planting became more rewarding than I could ever imagine. The excitement and joy of partnering with the Savior and King of the universe at every stage and step in the church planting process was simply indescribable.

Church planting presents the unique opportunity to explore Biblical Christianity in the community with fresh eyes. As the new congregation grows and develops intimacy in prayer, devotion to the things of God and a culture of church life; more knowledge and wisdom is received and cultivated in your heart and in the hearts of those who unit with you and join in the effort.

Church Planting is the design of God for the expansion of His Kingdom. Churches that catch the vision for church planting begin acting like the Church of the Scriptures. The establishment of the universal church and the multiplication of local churches is how God intends to accomplish His purpose of bringing glory to Himself. Uniting all things under Christ is the key to experiencing God's blessing. A Gospel-centered church multiplying is the plan of God, Himself. While planting churches is not easy, not cheap, and not without risk . . . Church planting is ordained by the very one who said, "Upon this rock, I will build my Church, and the gates of hell shall not prevail against it".

Developing a new church plant project can be extremely lonely at times and often there is little accountability for personal growth and time management. The Devil will take the opportunity to speak discouraging words or even find ways to hinder the church plant effort. Even spiritual leaders within the church planting arena can bring discouragement to the prospective planter. Learning to be self-disciplined is an essential characteristic for church planting developers. It is so important to stay in God's Word and cultivate a close and vibrant one-on-one relationship with the Savior who called you.

The Bible tells us that "unless the Lord builds the house, they labor in vain that build it." A very charismatic person can organize a great organization or club, but it is impossible for anyone to plant a church that is pleasing to God unless they rely on God to make it happen. Prayer is the act of admitting that God's will is done according to our faith. If the Lord is not directing the new church plant, then like Moses the church planter should refuse to continue the effort. The lesson to be learned is to always depend on our savior and creator for the wisdom to carry out His mission.

After praying and fasting for many days, God said, "move out" into the community. While walking the streets one day, I observed a single mother standing alone with her children. I was lead to ask her to let us, our church plant team, teach and mentor her children. The young mother reluctantly gave us permission to work with her children. In the beginning, financial resources were limited. The opportunity to become discouraged was very prevalent. Soon the group grew to seven and later on to twenty-five young children. As a result of continual fasting and prayer parents begin visiting the training sessions. Soon a Bible class was started. I continued to meet and share my vision with persons within the community. During the process, other supporters were added to the church planting team. They were people that I could count on for encouragement and shared vision. The group eventually grew to thirty persons. I soon realized that God was leading in ways that allowed us to form a church mission. The mission soon became a reality and eventually an established church. The name God gave for the church was Faith Tabernacle Church of Christ Holiness U.S.A. I praise God for His wonderful works that He has done. The mission church organized clothing giveaways, summer feeding programs, youth events, and healing and deliverance services. I thank God for blessing our effort with a strong church plant team, a permanent worship location and for the ability to provide support to those in need within the community.

When we are obedient and faithful to God's commands, He will reward us with the courage and influence we need to accomplish those things that He calls us to do. It is my desire that "Seeds for Harvest" will be a blessing to prospective church developers as they follow the strategic steps in planting and establishing a new church plant.

CHAPTER 1

VISION FOCUS AND STRATEGIC PLANNING

Church planting is one of the greatest and noblest of all spiritual undertakings. The prospective church planter must be equipped to meet the experience of such a challenging endeavor to advance the Kingdom of God. The vision must be focused and sure as to the direction God is leading.

As we look at the Apostle Paul's reason for planting churches; we must understand the prompting in each experience. It is clear in Acts 16 that the apostle Paul's motivation for going to Macedonia was a clear and compelling vision or revelation that he received from God. According to the Bible, in (Acts 16: 9), we are told that, "during the night Paul had a vision of a man of Macedonia standing and begging him, 'Come over to Macedonia and help us.' Immediately, Paul redirected his actions in response to that vision. As a result, the gospel was preached and a church was established at Philippi. Similarly, in the same way, church planting must flow out of a clear vision from God. Any other motivation, no matter how noble, is not sufficient. Therefore, it is essential that before church organizations or any church developer/pastor begins the journey of church planting there should be a clear understanding of what it means to receive a vision from God. The vision that Paul received was so specific and clear that it required a new direction. There was a new sense of authority in Paul's life. He was compelled toward this new vision. As a result Paul's obedience to God's leading allowed new converts to receive the Gospel message and new souls were added to the Kingdom of God. So it is with the effort of the church planter who should have a leading of the Holy Spirit and being strongly compelled to carry out God's vision for His church.

Discovering the Context of Shared Vision:

In order for the new vision to move forward it should be shared over and over again. Sharing the vision will become the catalyst for recruiting and gathering helpers for the cause of church planting. A simple definition of shared vision in a church planting context is: God's revelation of what He wants to accomplish in the reaching of a certain people group at a particular point in the future as a result of a church being faithfully and prayerfully planted.

The vision of the church plant is not created, for it already exists within the heart of God. Therefore, it is discovered as God reveals it to the listening church planter or church planting organization. This revealed vision must be shared by the church planter and followers of that vision. If this is the case, how does one go about discovering a shared vision? A shared vision is discovered over time and results from a number of different processes.

The following strategies are some common processes that can assist church planters in carrying out the process. Shared vision often begins with an intense burden owned by the church planter and affirmed by key individuals that has or will be recruited by the church planter. It reflects real needs among an unreached people. It is important that although the vision may begin with the church planter it is ultimately owned by a growing core of disciples or supporting team members. Any process utilized for discovering a shared vision must include those who join the planter in the mission of planting the church. Once a shared vision has been received, one has a foundation from which to proceed. All planning should follow a preparedness process. That is, instead of making plans and asking God to bless them, our plans should direct us toward activity that prepares us to respond to what God is doing.

Strategic preparedness focuses on aligning our lives in such a way that we can react to what God is doing around us. Strategic preparedness is not contrary to planning, but focuses on the type of planning we do. It forces us to direct our planning toward assuming a posture that can quickly respond to what God is doing around us and His invitation to join Him in the planting of His church.

There is no greater time to get involved in planting new churches. Starting new churches is the single greatest need and challenge facing believers in this nation. The revitalization of Christianity and the evangelization of our communities can only come about as a massive wave of new leaders is developed to establish and develop new faith communities. Why is church planting so important? The answer is simple: new churches are focused on the development of people.

New Churches Reach New People:

New churches are more effective than established churches at conversion growth," writes David T. Olson. "New churches often have three to four times the conversion rate that established churches do.' The cutting edge of evangelism around the world is church planting and the development of dynamic and new faith communities". If we are going to reach new people in our communities, church planting must be one of our highest priorities.

New Churches Challenge Young People:

Historically, we know that new churches are the best way for reaching a new generation. Each generation needs its own new type of church that speaks the gospel in a new and fresh way. Taking the unchanging substance of our message and adapting the way we communicate it to the style and values of a younger group of people is increasingly necessary in the 21st century.

New Churches Connect Diverse People:

America is growing more diverse with each passing year. New churches are able to connect with that diversity in ways that current or traditional churches do not. It seems that every people group needs to hear the gospel in a way that connects with its own culture and context. New churches start with a "clean slate" and are able to attract a diverse population without barriers.

New Churches Revitalize God's People:

The birth of new churches helps an established congregation "feel young again." Just like a proud grandparent says, "My grandchildren really keep me on my toes," so it is when a mature congregation helps to give birth to a new congregation. The vitality and excitement of the daughter church rubs off on the mother church, and the maturity and experience of the mother deeply influences the daughter!

New Churches Mobilize Committed People:

For various reasons people who are committed to and active participants in an established church are often not being used to their full potential as leaders. The development of new worship venues, new church sites, and new congregations can be a force for mobilizing these vital people. New opportunities for leadership and creativity abound in a new and growing church and many people find that even temporary involvement in a new church can strengthen their gifts for ministry.

It is so important that we find the courage to move out of our comfort zone and allow God to use us in a different way. In Genesis

12:1-4, God gave Abram a revelation of what He wanted to accomplish in and through him. "The Lord had said to Abram, 'Leave your country, your people and your father's household and go to the land I will show you. I will make you into a great nation and I will bless you; I will make your name great, and you will be a blessing. I will bless those who bless you, and whoever curses you I will curse; and all peoples on earth will be blessed through you.' So Abram left, as the Lord had told him; and Lot went with him. Abram was seventy-five years old when he set out from Haran."

Notice Abram's response to God's revelation. Abram simply left and did what the Lord revealed to him. A good question to consider is, "If God revealed a new thing to us in relationship to what He wants to accomplish in and through us, how long would it take us to get in a position to respond?" Once again, Spiritual preparedness is about positioning ourselves or assuming a posture that frees us to respond to God's activity around us. When following a preparedness process there are a number of components that make up a shared vision. They include:

- *Vision Statement*—a vision statement flows out of your overall vision and serves as a means to communicate "what" God has called you to become as a church.
- *Mission Statement*—a mission statement describes "How you are to accomplish the vision that is the "what."
- *Core Values*—Core values are deep-seated convictions that drive behavior. While vision serves to ignite us, core values tend to unite us. They become the shared beliefs that are acted out in our daily behavior as a community committed to a common vision and mission.
- *System Design*—describes the strategic process by which we accomplish our vision and mission. It also defines the relationships of the individual components to the whole.

The planter receives a vision that clearly reveals what God wants to accomplish. The planter then must determine the major spiritual preparation needed in order to prepare and to respond to God's continual activity in planting His church. When there is shared vision of all involved and supporters who will embrace the vision, we are better prepared to respond to what our Heavenly Father is leading us to do.

We must be sure we are following God's will in all things. Only God knows what is best for us. Only He knows what will work and what will not work. And only God knows the future. Therefore, only by following God's guidance can we be sure of success.

The question of who is in authority must be answered first. Many churches use the pyramid type organization, where the senior minister is at the top with assistant ministers under him and a board of elders or deacons under them. The work is done through various programs, such as a calling program, music program, youth program, Sunday school program, sports programs, etc. These programs do not obtain the results God expects of us, because they do not change people into the likeness of Christ but can attract the interest of certain groups who can be drawn to Christ.

In a religious organization chart, Jesus Christ should be at the top of the top. God uses all of them working together in various ways, methods, and techniques. How God does His work is so complicated that it is beyond our understanding. Our part is to be under the authority of Christ and under the authority of those He has put over us. Then, we can perform the ministry He gives us. We do not need to go looking for a ministry, for if we allow God to make us usable, He will use us.

"Now to him who is able to do exceedingly abundantly above all that we ask or think, according to the power that works in us, to him be the glory in the assembly and in Christ Jesus to all generations forever and ever. Amen." Ephesians 3:20, 21.

Knowing God's Will:

Much of God's will is revealed to us in the Bible, yet there are people who know the Bible but do not understand God's will for their lives or ministry. Others claim the Holy Spirit guides them but the fruit they produce is not the fruit of the Holy Spirit. How can we be sure that we are not like them? How can we avoid the mistakes we see others make? The answer is not simple for God works in many ways to perform His work. A study of those Jesus healed reveal that each healing was different. A study of the conversions in the New Testament reveals that the people became Christians in different ways. No two circumstances happened in exactly the same way. The way God calls one person into a ministry and the way he calls another may be in entirely different ways and for different types of work.

God Guides Us Through:

The Bible is God's road map for us. It will take you where God wants you to go if you are willing to study it and allow God to give you wisdom to understand His ways. "But if any of you lacks wisdom, let him ask of God, who gives to all liberally and without reproach; and it will be given to him. But let him ask in faith, without any doubting, for he who doubts is like a wave of the sea, driven by the wind and tossed. For let that man not thinks that he will receive anything from the Lord." James 1:5-7. "For the word of God is living, and active, and sharper than any two-edged sword, and piercing even to the dividing of soul and spirit, of both joints and marrow, and is able to discern the thoughts and intentions of the heart." (Hebrews 4:12).

Dedication:

We cannot learn God's will until we completely dedicate ourselves to God. This includes our body, soul, spirit, time, possessions and family.

It means giving up the desire to do our own thing. The more we dedicate ourselves to God the greater will be our ability to know and understand God's will.

Paul says, "Therefore I urge you, brethren, by the mercies of God, to present your bodies a living sacrifice, holy, acceptable to God, which is your reasonable service, and be not conformed to this world, but be ye transformed by the renewing of your mind, that ye may prove what is the good and acceptable and perfect will of God." (Romans 12:1-2)

Finances:

God will provide the funds for any ministry He calls us to. At times God guides us by providing or withholding funds for a work we are doing. If God has not provided funds then we are either on the wrong track, or going ahead of God, or He is testing our faith. An assembly must avoid going into debt if possible, selling items to raise money, begging for money, or using gimmicks to acquire money. How can God guide us if we use these methods to fund our work? Whenever a Christian ministry or assembly begs for money, that ministry should reexamine the vision and focus.

Often God will not reveal His future plans to us, for if He did we are likely to run ahead of Him, trying to do His work with our own energy and wisdom. Therefore, it is usually difficult to budget for future expenses of an assembly. By faith we know that God will provide. Those in charge of establishing must pray to God for directions. God knows the future so He knows what funds will be needed. Therefore a church of tithing members will have no financial problems. (See 2 Corinthians 9:6-15)

A Vision:

Sometimes God will give us a special vision of a ministry He wants accomplished. If God gives you a vision, you must not expect the death of that vision even if events happen that make it seem impossible to accomplish. God in His own time will perform the vision through you in ways beyond your greatest expectations. When you think the vision is dead and you see no way it can be accomplished you must not doubt, for God will keep His promise if we are faithful. Abraham and the birth of Isaac is a wonderful example. Many days passed before God fulfilled the promise of a son.

The Holy Spirit:

To know God's will we must know His Word and listening to the promptings of the Holy Spirit. We have the Holy Spirit living in us, who communicates with our spirit. If our fleshly nature is controlling our life, we will have difficulty hearing the communication between our spirit and the Holy Spirit. When our spirit is in control of our life, we will hear the promptings of the Holy Spirit. The Holy Spirit will prompt you through reading the Bible, through the authorities He has put over you, through fervent prayer, and through direct communication. "And your ears shall hear a word behind you, saying, this is the way, walk you in it; when you turn to the right hand, and when you turn to the left." Isaiah 30:21. Extreme care must be used in hearing the voice of the Holy Spirit, for Satan can also put thoughts in your head. The difference is that Satan always misuses God's Word, while the Holy Spirit always agrees with it.

Often God's direction is one step at a time. He will direct you to take the first step, but only after you take that step will He direct you for the next step. As you go one step at a time you will then find the direction God is guiding you. "A man's heart plans his course, but God directs his steps." (Proverbs 16:9).

Prayer:

Prayer is how we communicate with God, while God's Word is His chief communication with us. For a Church to be successful its members must become effective in prayer. Successful prayer depends upon the following:

Prayer of Faith:

"Jesus answering said to them, "Have faith in God. For most assuredly I tell you, whoever may tell this mountain, 'Be taken up and cast into the sea,' and doesn't doubt in his heart, but believes that what he says is happening; he shall have whatever he says. Therefore I tell you, all things whatever you pray and ask for, believe that you receive them, and you shall have them." (Mark 11:22-24). Honest and true faith is the test to believe that God is able to not only meet our every need but hear and answer our prayers.

Pray With Proper Motive:

"You ask, and don't receive, because you ask amiss, so that you may spend it for your pleasures." James 4:3. Implement a personal prayer walk as you develop ways of exercising your faith to receive a positive response to your prayers.

Prayer of Obedience:

Let us bring our hearts into obedience to God; "Beloved, if our hearts don't condemn us, we have boldness toward God; and whatever we ask, we receive from him, because we keep his commandments and do the things that are pleasing in his sight. This is his commandment, that we should believe in the name of his Son, Jesus Christ, and love one another, even as he commanded. He who keeps his commandments remains in him, and he in him. By this we know that he remains in us, by the Spirit which he gave us." (1 John 3:21-24).

Asking In God's Will:

We must open our hearts to the will of God. If God said it, He can accomplish it; that settles it: "This is the boldness which we have toward him, that, if we ask anything according to his will, he hears us. And if we know that he hears us, whatever we ask, we know that we have the petitions which we have asked of him." (1 John 5:14, 15).

Praying In the Name of Jesus:

We must ask in faith and we will receive it; according to God's Word. "Whatever you will ask in my name, that will I do, that the Father may be glorified in the Son. If you will ask anything in my name, I will do it." (John 14:13, 14).

Circumstances:

At times God will bring people into our lives that we are to help. This may consist of offering friendship, spiritual counsel, encouragement, or meeting their physical needs. We must follow God's leading and the prompting of the Holy Spirit in deciding whom to help. We must be willing to help those whom God brings across our paths. The Good Samaritan is our example. Yet we are commanded to not help or associate with those who call themselves Christian but do not live a Christ like life style. These are listed in (1 Corinthians 5:11, Romans 16:17, 18; and 2 Timothy 3:1-5).

"He also said to the one, who had invited him, 'When you make a dinner or a supper, don't call your friends, nor your brothers, nor your kinsmen, nor rich neighbors, or perhaps they might also return the favor, and pay you back. But when you make a feast, ask the poor, the maimed, the lame, or the blind; and you will be blessed, because they don't have the resources to repay you. For you will be repaid in the resurrection of the righteous.'" (Luke 14:12-14). One major difference in church planting is that you will be going to persons who perhaps never believed in Jesus or any religious experience. In the above passage the church planting personality is described.

CHAPTER 2

DEFINING AND TARGETING DEMOGRAPHIC POPULATIONS

An effective new church development team must define its target area and audience. At the same time, God's church is open to all comers, but few churches if any can be all things to all people, especially new church plants. Throughout the Scriptures, God declares His love and eternal purposes with a focus on identifiable groupings of people worldwide. In Genesis, God makes a covenant with the family of Abraham in order to bless all families of the earth. In Matthew, God commands His disciples to make disciples of all groups of people in the world. In Revelation, God reveals that heaven will be populated with people from every tribe, tongue, and race. God created many cultures containing many ways for people to group themselves. These social structures allow the gospel of Jesus Christ to move rapidly from group to group through natural and familiar relationships. Effective church planters will focus on a specific group or segment of people; and, thereby, take advantage of God's design to grow His kingdom through engaging every significant grouping of people in every society. This process of focusing on a specific group of people is called defining your church planting focus group.

Targeting and defining a target group requires strategic planning. For example, when you distribute flyers for vacation Bible school, you go to neighborhoods with children, and avoid the retirement community. When you are trying to attract youth groups, you could possibly put ads for special church concerts in the local newspaper. Target evangelism is not an attempt to exclude anyone. Rather, it is a method that helps churches deal better with economic realities. Most churches do not have the resources to provide programs for every demographic or generational group of people. If you can afford to minister to everyone, then do so. If you are working with a limited budget or none at all, you must decide who you will target with your message.

Sociographic Targeting:

Using the U. S. Census information can help a church planting team define the sociographic groups in its ministry area. Using U.S. Census Bureau information, provide a demographic breakdown of an area that includes age, income, population change, race, and what it calls "U.S. lifestyle segments." By overlaying information gathered from its surveys on lifestyle segments, can help the church plant team strategically decide on church programs, faith, worship, music, and advertising methods.

A church plant team leader can ask for demographic reports according to zip codes, a specific radius around its building, or a specific area it has defined in the community. The package of information the church receives includes a description of how the data were gathered, an explanation of the characteristics of the U.S. lifestyle segments.

Other strategies such as social media may be employed such as the use of high-tech resources to learn about other target groups. This strategy may be used to gain insight into new ways to reach the un-churched. New technology can in some ways compete with such strategies as knocking on doors and passing out evangelistic tracks.

Generational Targeting:

One way to understand the people in a potential ministry field is to view them as members of a unique generation. People who lived through the Depression, for example, operate differently from people who came of age during the Vietnam conflict. As we study the population, you will find that baby boomers have different goals and beliefs than recent college graduates who are just beginning their careers. Christian publishing houses are producing resources to help churches get a handle on generational issues. Many of those resources are targeted for the following generations:

<u>Bridgers</u>—describes the Post Generation Xers:

The post-Xers are the bridge to the 21st century. According to researchers, a high percentage of Bridgers attend church, but low percentages making commitments to Christ. To encourage more commitments, churches should put more emphasis on children and youth evangelism, not just youth programs. In addition to identifying the tendencies of this generation, churches should make an intentional effort to be Bridger-friendly.

Generation X:

Generation X refers to young adults in our culture. We must not make assumptions about individuals based upon trends of a generational group and the power of God to impact their lives. Developing strong young adult ministries is the key to reaching this segment of the population.

One of the most popular used strategies for ministering to young adults are big events, challenging discipleship courses, small groups, and music ministries.

Baby Boomers:

In order to reach the older population, churches must deliberately become family centered. When ministries provide opportunities for older adults to use their knowledge and experience they reconnect with the fiber of the community. Seniors can be used in the churches marriage mentoring events as an example to younger couples who may experience difficulty in their marriages. I believe older members will enjoy being advisors for younger couples as they share their experiences of life.

Builders:

Senior adult ministry can become the key to reenergize the connection between the church and seniors citizens. An effort should be made to create ways to sustain an on-going relationship with senior adults. A good strategy for outreach is to recruit seniors to work in peer-friendship evangelism, revivals, newcomer visitation, and integrating church visitors into church programs.

How to Hit the Target:

Churches can use traditional means of advertising, such as direct mail, the newspaper, or yellow pages to reach a generational target with their message. However, there is another, more personal approach. In metropolitan areas, two types of churches are emerging. The neighborhood church ministers to people within a certain radius of the church. A regional church draws members from all over the city. The congregation must thus rethink the notion of attracting people who live near the church. One way to deal with this is to target people in the neighborhoods of church members rather than in the area around the church.

Other ideas for targeting individuals for the church:

Prayer: *Prayer* to help Christians learn to pray like Jesus prayed so they can live as He lived. It includes an in-depth study of Jesus' prayer life and some tools to help people organize their prayer life and keep track of prayer requests. Locate workbooks that teach Christians how to pray for non-believing neighbors, friends, and family members.

Reach out to those that are hungry:

Feeding the hungry is a strategy to cultivate relationships in a neighborhood by collecting canned foods for a hunger drive. This program helps feed the hungry, gives Christians reason to knock on their neighbors' doors, and builds relationships. A neighborhood prayer captain gathers the food, and then returns the next month to thank neighbors for their contributions and to report on how much food the neighborhood collected. While they are calling on neighbors, prayer captains can gather prayer needs.

Neighborhood evangelism mobilizes church members to take spiritual responsibility for their neighbors. In the process, they build positive relationships, increase the visibility of the church's prayer ministry, make a priority of talking to God about a person before talking to a person about God, help the community work on solving the hunger problem, and present the gospel in a nonthreatening way.

Though a church may select a target group to evangelize, it should also be ready to minister to whoever walks through its doors. I am always encouraged when reading the promised God made to Abraham and other servants in the bible. God is insuring His servant that He will be with him. "Now the Lord said to Abram: "I will bless those who bless you, and I will curse him who curses you; and in you all the families of the earth shall be blessed" (Gen. 12:1-3).

Ministering to the Un-Churched:

I believe building relationships with people can be one of the best ways of drawing people to your church. Someone said, "People don't care how much you know, until they know how much you care." While seeking to establish our church, we surveyed the community in order to discover what the needs and interests were in the community. We soon discovered it was a perfect way not only for individuals to know who we were but also a good way to share our vision. Un-churched individuals need our care and attention. Some of the questions on our survey were as follows: What encourages a person to come to church? What makes them stay? The answers to these questions gave us insight into the mind of un-churched persons and gave us guidance in reaching them more effectively. Some of the answers to the questions above are as follows:

What Makes Them Come?

We found that the reasons the formerly un-churched chose a particular church were complex. But while the teaching and the personality of the pastor are a leading factor for selecting a church, relationships play a key role in helping the un-churched make their initial church visit.

We found that almost four out of ten of the formerly un-churched indicated that family members were important in their choice of a church. Some said that relationships other than family members brought them to church. Studies shows that about 73 percent of individuals interviewed revealed the importance of a relationship in their choice of a church. Although our study survey affirms how important relationships are in reaching the un-churched, it indicates that other factors are just as important such as visitors recognizing that church members care for those who visit them.

Being a Living Example:

It is so important that leaders in the church live the life that they preach, teach and sing about. But more important are other factors listed below which are as follows:

Here are a few to consider:

- Helping and referring persons through severe crises in their lives
- The in-home visits by the pastor and church members
- Scheduling major events and inviting individuals to come.
- The personal evangelistic witness of a church member
- The relationship of a friend
- The friendliness of the church members
- The preaching of the pastor

As you can see relationships are only part of the answer; while the appeal of a pastor or relationships are important to bringing someone in the door of a church, the reasons people stay at a church are very different. Our survey revealed the following factors.

1. We found that a combination of ministry involvement helps to grow the church.
2. Sunday school and obedience to God topped the list of reasons why they stayed active at the church.
3. Again, while we can't discount the value of fellowship, the formerly un-churched told us that their service and ministry in the church kept them coming back each week more than any other factor.
4. Relationships will bring people in the door, good preaching will influence church selection, but connection through volunteer ministry is the most important long term factor for maintaining church involvement.

We must also stand on the promises that Jesus gave to His followers, "And Jesus came and spoke to them, saying, 'All authority has been given to me in heaven and on earth. Go therefore and make disciples of all the nations, baptizing them in the name of the Father and of the Son and of the Holy Spirit, teaching them to observe all things that I have commanded you; and lo I am with you always, even to the end of the age' (Matt. 28:18-20). Kingdom workers should be encouraged as they step out in faith to meet the challenge of establishing God's ministry.

CHAPTER 3

RECRUITING A CHURCH PLANTING TEAM

According to the Bible, one of the first actions taken by the apostle Paul in his church planting ministry was to share with a team the vision God had given him. Notice the "we" and "us" of Acts 16:10, "After Paul had seen the vision; we got ready at once to leave for Macedonia, concluding that God had called us to preach the gospel to them" (Acts 16:10). Without question, starting a biblically functioning congregation requires a team effort. But what is a team? A team is "a group of people bound together by a commitment to reach a shared goal." Thus, a team can be a group of professional football players who strive to win the Super Bowl. It can be a group of Sunday school teachers who pour their lives into middle school students. It can be a group of people who start a church for the purpose of carrying out Christ's Great Commission in their community and around the world.

If possible, the church planting team should be formed months ahead of the actual church plant. It will depend on the organizing religious institution that should participate in the new church start planning process. The church plant team should consist of several key individuals. These individuals include the planter's spouse (if married), a parent church representative, a mentor or mentors, and individual prayer intercessors.

The planter is ready to move forward when all of these are in place.

The church planter's spouse is critical to the church planting process. If the planter's spouse is not on board; the church planter should not qualify for the church planting task. The planter and his spouse must have a strong and growing relationship, because church planting is a stressful endeavor that can tax even the best marriage.

A New Testament pattern for church planting should include a sending or parenting organization.. Paul went to Jerusalem prior to his first missionary journey. From day one of his church planting activity, Paul was sent out and supported by the Jerusalem church. The Antioch church later became an important sending church for Paul, but he was always connected to a sending or parenting church.

Paul not only had a sending church, but he also had a mentor, Barnabas. Every Church planter will greatly benefit from a mentor or mentors who encourage and offer them healthy spiritual advice along the way. Successful church planters should be great discerners and have a teachable spirit that is most often demonstrated in their practice of seeking out mentors. It is good advice for church planters to meet weekly or as often as possible for advice or just means of fellowship. When these protocols are not established the church organizer has no option but to find other funding opportunities to use personal resources to see the new plant effort through. This suggests that those who are teachable and seek out the wise instruction of others tend to translate their learning into results. Prior to starting a church, a planter also needs to identify individual prayer intercessors. One can't begin to communicate the importance of a committed group of intercessors. This team should consist of individuals committed to praying regularly and intentionally for the church planter, his spouse and children, and his ministry.

When the initial church planting team is in place, the church planter is ready to start the process of discovering a church planting strategy. Most church planting strategies call for the formation of other ministry teams to work together with the church planting team. Several types of supplemental teams may be utilized in planting the church. Some of these teams are briefly described below.

Understanding the Role of Church Planting Teams:

The church planting team is of ultimate importance if the church plant process is going to be successful. Other teams may be needed beyond those listed here. However, the teams described here are commonly used by many church planters today. A staff team's primary role is to equip the core group to provide the basic ministry of the church plant. This team may consist of two or more individuals committed to work together in the planting and leading of the new church.

When a staff team is used to plant a church, it usually consists of a lead pastor, a worship leader, and/or a pastor of spiritual development. In the beginning the lead pastor may share several roles. The team may or may not share the preaching and teaching, but all are responsible for equipping and growing a church plant in a given context. Paul put it this way: "It was he who gave some to be apostles, some to be prophets, some to be evangelists, and some to be pastors and teachers, to prepare God's people for works of service, so that the body of Christ may be built up until we all reach unity in the faith and in the knowledge of the Son of God and become mature attaining to the whole measure of the fullness of Christ" (Eph. 4:11-13).

A core group's primary role is to become the expression of Christ in the ministry.

It is the vehicle through which the sharing of a common vision, values, mission, and strategies take place. The core group exercises their gifts in carrying out the Great Commandment and Great Commission in the planting of a church. Again, it is the role of the church planter or staff team to equip this core group for the many responsibilities of planting the church. This core group may consist of people from a parenting church or the community. It will often consist of people at various spiritual levels. Sometimes those who are exploring Christianity for the first time can play a role in the core group.

A ministry team should consist of core group members organized to carry out a specific task. Ministry teams usually consist of a leader and several other team members who meet regularly to plan and carry out a particular ministry of the church. Most church plants will require several different ministry teams. Each of these teams will consist of individuals who have gathered to accomplish a specific ministry task. Such tasks may include set up and break down for the service, leading in worship, providing child care, running audio/visual equipment, leading small groups, greeting, visitor follow-up, and so on.

A leadership team may consist of members of the staff as well as members of the core group. Some structures take the leaders from the ministry teams and develop a leadership team out of that group. A key role of the leadership team is to provide spiritual direction and accountability for the church plant while overseeing that the vision, values, mission, and strategy are being carried out. This team can be invaluable when it comes to developing a leadership structure for the church. However, developing a team around trust, vision, values, and a common mission takes time. In a new church, individuals tend to come and go. Therefore, it is important not to organize a permanent leadership structure too early.

Characteristics of a Team:

Regardless of the type of team you are working with, there are some processes that is important to developing healthy teams. This process begins with creating a sense of togetherness. Most people long to be part of something that is far greater than themselves. This longing can forge a bond of unity among team members. This sense of togetherness takes place when every team member feels that they are making a unique contribution to the team. Different people with different spiritual gifts, experiences, relational styles, and ministry skills are needed for a church planting team to be complete.

Additionally, a sense of togetherness grows as people commit themselves to a team's shared goals. Jesus insisted that if a person wanted to follow Him, he or she must share His values and goals. He said, "He who is not with me is against me, and he who does not gather with me scatters" (Matt. 12:30). Jesus made sure that anyone who wanted to be on His team was committed to His mission.

Secondly, an effective church planter builds a team by empowering others to lead.

John Maxwell has observed a great irony of leadership: "If you want to do something really big that involves a lot of people; you need to narrow your focus to a few people." Leaders who lead leaders must share their power. The apostle Paul multiplied his ministry by multiplying leaders, not by gathering followers. He started with a few potential leaders, and he committed his life to helping them reach their leadership potential. Because he did, the first-century church experienced exponential growth like the world had never seen.

Thirdly, a church planter builds a team through accountability. It is only after a team comes together and is fully empowered to accomplish its mission that accountability comes into play. The environment for good accountability is one that is forged over time through an open and honest trust relationship. Trust equals accountability; therefore, the higher the degree of trust, the higher the accountability. Accountability consists of team members' strong desire not to drop the ball or let down the team and willingness for the team leader to see every team member succeed. Healthy teams are the context for accountability. When this process is followed it allows the team to experience success.

Fourthly, church planting leaders become successful when they have mentored a successor to carry on the mission of the team. According to Maxwell, "There is no success without a successor." In every successful church plant and team ministry, the leader mentors others who will continue the mission long after the leader is gone. Mentoring is how leaders prepare the next generation of leaders for service. Without future leaders, there is no future for the church or ministry. Jesus, the ultimate mentor, mentored His followers in at least three ways. First, He mentored His disciples by teaching them. He taught them through stories, parables, and object lessons how to live in the kingdom of God. Second, Jesus mentored His followers by revealing the power of God in their lives (Mark 6:32-44). Jesus was building the faith of the disciples by His miracles. Thirdly, Jesus mentored His disciples by modeling and teaching them a life of prayer (Luke 11:1-4).

The Importance of Teams in Church Planting:

Church planting teams are invaluable when it comes to starting a need ministry. One church planter made a statement about his responsibility, he explained, "God has not called me here to plant a church. He has called me here to gather a group of people and equip them to plant a church." Clearly, Paul believed that team ministry would prove more effective over the long run than his individual efforts.

When a church planter utilizes his team he can:

- Multiply ministry;
- Mentor others;
- Maximize resources and
- Mobilize the body.

Enlisting Team Members:

1. When we seek to recruit team members we should follow the words of Jesus; we should pray. Jesus said, "The harvest is plentiful but the laborers are few. Pray the God of the harvest to send out workers into His harvest" (Matt. 9:37-38). It is amazing that 2,000 years ago Jesus knew the number one need

would be for workers for the harvest field. With this in mind, He instructed us to pray for workers. Nothing will substitute for prayer when it comes to building solid ministry teams. Pray for God to lead you to people of solid character who are committed to Christ, to God's vision for Kingdom Building.

2. Seek to empower those who share your vision. List tasks and define roles needed to accomplish the vision God has given you for your community. Know what you need before you begin looking for someone. This will enable you to begin to pray specifically for future team members. John Maxwell has compiled a list of "Top 20 Personal Requirements" he looks for in potential staff members. Many of the requirements for leaders focus on their character. Traits such as integrity, responsible, flexible, creative, disciplined, and resilient are indispensable for church planting team members.

3. Look for ways that God may be answering your prayers. It is always important to be aware of the people God is bringing into your life every day. Remember That God often works through the network of relationships you are building. As you pray over specific individuals, ask them to introduce you to people in their network who might share a burden to help start a church.

4. Personally invite individuals to join you in your church planting endeavor. I have learned from experience in church planting to; first, the people you need typically are the people who don't need you. They are busy people because they get things done. Thus, they are not looking to fill up their schedule. You must go looking for them. Second, sharp people rarely volunteer to do anything. However, they generally will do whatever you personally ask them to do.

5. As you spend time with people, listen to them and observe them *over* time, you will learn what ministries they feel most passionate about and what ministries bring them the most fulfillment.

6. *Equip and release people for service*: Develop some kind of leadership structure and process that allows you to provide ongoing equipping. This equipping may take one of two forms: as-you-go equipping and intentional equipping. Early in a church plant you will need to spend regular time with your team preparing them for the task. However, over time, their equipping needs will change. Some church planters set aside a monthly time with ministry team leaders; others set aside time for a major equipping event two or three times a year.
7. *Monitor the team's progress monthly and mentor them as needed.* Keep in touch with your teams. It is important that you spend time with key leaders. The ministry of presence goes a long way in keeping teams motivated and encouraged. A good friend offers a key shepherding idea. He suggests that a church planter or pastor always leave early when he is headed somewhere on or off campus in order to connect with people as he traveled to the destination.
8. Encourage teams often and celebrate the victories, both great and small. Look for intentional ways to celebrate positive team behavior and victories. As you develop your goals look for opportunities to create small wins. Affirm people publicly and privately.

Servant Leadership:

For a church planter to be most effective, he must develop a "whatever-it takes no-matter-who-gets-the-credit" attitude. People are quick to follow those who love them and are willing to lay down their life for them. A church planter must resist the temptation to drive people and come to understand that the key to leadership is humility.

Servanthood:

The apostle Paul, arguably is one of the greatest church planter and ministry team leader in history, offered some tips on how to make ministry teams work over the long haul. According to, Colossians 3:12-14, he writes: "Therefore, as God's chosen people, holy and dearly loved, clothe yourselves with compassion, kindness, humility, gentleness and patience. Bear with each other and forgive whatever grievances you may have against one another. Forgive as the Lord forgave you. And over these virtues put on love, which binds them all together in perfect unity."

This passage reminds us that unconditional surrender by the planter and his team produces undeniable transformation and an unstoppable church. Perhaps it would serve any church planter well to understand that as a servant leader he is responsible for (1) setting direction, (2) creating a healthy environment, and (3) serving his team. It is not unusual for the most successful church planters to understand that it is their role to serve the team, not the team's to serve them.

CHAPTER 4

BEGIN WITH AN END IN MIND: IDENTIFYING RESOURCES

It is very important that the church planter count up the cost. Since God created everything, it becomes necessary that we pray to God for what we need. The Bible commands us to ask for what we need. "Ask and it will be given to you; seek and you will find; knock and it will be opened; "for everyone who asks receives; he who seeks finds; and to him who knocks, the door will be opened" (Matt.7:7-8). "Suppose one of you wants to build a tower. Will he not first sit down and estimate the cost to see if he has enough money to complete it? For if he lays the foundation and is not able to finish it, everyone who sees it will ridicule him, saying, 'this fellow began to build and was not able to finish'" (Luke 14:28-30).

"In the church at Antioch there were prophets and teachers: Barnabas, Simeon called Niger, Lucius of Cyrene, Manaen (who has been brought up with Herod the Tetrarch) and Saul. While they were worshiping the Lord and fasting, the Holy Spirit said, 'Set apart for Me Barnabas and Paul for the work to which I have called them.' So after they had fasted and prayed, they placed their hands on them and sent them off" (Acts 13:1-3).

In Luke 14:28-30, Jesus very clearly communicates the importance of counting the cost prior to beginning a venture. Often times organized churches may not have all of the necessary funds to plant a mission ministry. It may require great sacrifice by the church planter and his family to continue the process. So this is sometimes the case for the church planter who truly has the vision to carry out the church planting process. Church planting can be a costly venture that requires significant resourcing. There are two basic types of resources that exist in any church plant: people resources and financial resources.

People Resources:

As one studies the New Testament pattern for church planting three relational strategies are emphasized. The biblical pattern suggests that a church planter has a relationship with a sending church, he works in relationship to a team, and he has a significant relationship with a mentor or an experienced pastor or developer.

- *Sending Church*—the church at Antioch serves as a prime example of a sending church. Key principles related to the importance of a sending church are found in Acts 13:1-3.

    The church at Antioch was compelled by the Holy Spirit to send both Paul and Barnabas as an extension of their responsibility to fulfilling the Great Commission (v. 2). They intentionally set Paul and Barnabas aside for this work and sent them off to accomplish this task. This implies an ongoing relationship and responsibility between the church planter and the sending church (vv. 2-3).
- *Team*—the Antioch church set Paul and Barnabas apart and sent them off as part of a team. This pattern began with our Lord modeling team ship and continued throughout the New Testament. Mark 3:13-15 gives us insight into Jesus' commitment to building teams: "Jesus went up on a mountainside and called

to him those he wanted, and they came to him. He appointed twelve—designating them apostles—that they might be with him and that he might send them out to preach and to have authority to drive out demons."

- *Mentor*—Although Barnabas was a team member, his relationship with Paul began as an encourager and sponsor, two primary functions of a mentor. Like Paul, church planters must be learners. There is a great need to have someone to be a listener in times of challenge.

Financial Resources:

In addition to the right people resources, financial resources must be considered.

The type and amount of these resources required depends on the planter's approach and philosophy of church planting. It is not uncommon for a potential church planter to ask the question, "How much will it cost?" Although the remainder of this chapter discusses financial resources, remember that people resources are just as important, if not more important, than financial resources.

How much will it cost?

1. *It will cost more than you think.* Regardless of the type of church you are planting, chances are it will cost more than you think. Successful planters need to pay close attention to the identification of resources. No church will be planted without personal sacrifice. It has been the experience of many that one's vision always outpaces resources; therefore, cost must be considered, and ongoing efforts to raise resources are necessary.

2. *It depends on the type of church you plant.* For the sake of this discussion, even though there are many different approaches

and models of church planting, we will look at two approaches: traditional church plants and nontraditional church plants.

- *Traditional church plants*—those that typically require a meeting place and a paid church planter. Their style of ministry may or may not be traditional, but they take on a more institutional form with a very organized structure. They usually require a large amount of financial resourcing or a bi-vocational staff.
- *Nontraditional church plants*—those that are typically more organic than organized. They may meet in houses, storefronts, office buildings, apartments, or clubhouses. They are often lay-led or led by a pastor who doesn't need a salary. They focus on multiplying and expanding through small networks. They often require very little funding; however, they do require a high level of commitment.

3. *It depends on the vision.* In the planting of any church, one must begin with the end in mind. If God is leading one to an unreached people who will require a more institutional form of church, it may require a large amount of resources from day one. However, it is important to understand that the more resources you put into a church does not guarantee a given outcome. One church planter had $10,000 committed by a parenting church. The planter spent about $6,000 in pre-launch types of activities that included marketing, a used sound system, signs, and nursery and preschool equipment. On opening day, 178 people attended. Today, the church has over 2,000 worship attendees on a given weekend. This church has also planted a number of churches.

When there is little or no support in bringing a vision into reality, there must be other strategies to get the church planting activity started. Today, there seems to be an emerging vision for planting lay-led churches that require little financial resourcing. These churches usually meet in homes, coffee shops, boardrooms, and apartments. By design, they stay small, but focus on multiplying themselves through a growing network of missional lay leadership.

This emerging vision seems to be embraced by a young, postmodern culture and may be the antitheses of the highly organized and institutionalized mega-church.

4. *It depends on the type of launch.* There are a variety of ways to plant a new congregation that impacts the amount of financial resources needed. The more believers you have in the core group the less likely you will need to focus on a high-cost launch strategy. If believers are taught to share their faith and are actively building relationships in the un-churched community, growth can be fast and sure through networking. If the planter is in a highly un-churched context and has a traditional church planting strategy with a small believer base, his start-up strategies will likely have to depend on ministry evangelism events and an effective marketing plan. Both of these approaches can be costly.

Another factor likely to impact the cost of start-up is the rental cost of a meeting location. If the launch strategy is to attract a large group of people, it will require a meeting place that can handle the crowd. A space for 200 people in worship can require a large amount of financial resourcing. However, a home, coffee shop, or boardroom usually doesn't cost anything and opens up an entire relational network.

5. *It depends on the context of your ministry.* Socioeconomic factors have a dramatic impact on the individual's values. What one group may see as wasteful, another sees as the cost of doing business. When one's church planting focus group represents a higher socioeconomic group it will require more financial

resourcing. Limited resourcing could spell doom from day one. There are a lot of factors that play into this aspect of resourcing. Careful consideration should be given to the issue of context.

6. *It depends on the planter's unique gifts and talents.* Every planter is unique and will approach the task of planting based on his spiritual gifts, heart, ability, personality, and experiences. One planter may find that he is task-oriented with an administrative gift and a business background. He may tend to approach church planting from an organizational perspective. He is likely to create a start-up strategy similar to the launching of a new business. Also, a church planter may be highly relational and his start-up strategy may reflect a more organic approach to church planting.

What Do I Need?

Many ways exist to break down the basic financial needs a planter has as the process of planning occurs to plant a church. There seem to be three basic needs: a start-up budget, an operational budget, and salary support. Breaking the financial needs down into these three categories is beneficial when it comes to raising support. For example, some people give financial support based on relationship. These individuals will most likely be drawn to give to support the planter's salary. Other individuals like to give a gift to meet a concrete need, like a video projector. The core group and growing number of attendees will likely want to give toward the ongoing
 operation of the new church. Dividing gifts—giving—into these three categories organizes the needs into manageable categories.

A start-up budget consists of those things required for launching a new church.

These items include initial marketing strategy, worship equipment, nursery and preschool equipment, rental deposits, insurance, signs, letterhead, bulletin cover, and so forth. Some of these items will be included later in operational costs, but are also part of the initial start-up cost.

The operation budget consists of those things that recur and make up an annual budget. These items should fall into such categories as missions, personnel, facilities, administration, and ministry. It is important to build good financial systems from day one. When you are establishing your first operational budget, there are a number of things to consider:

- Establish an account in the church's name.
- Handle the finances as quickly as possible.
- Establish financial guidelines.
- Designate someone to handle the money. As planter/pastor make an attempt never to handle the money.
- Use two signatures for checks.
- Have an outside audit conducted annually.
- Budget with the end in mind.
- Maintain flexibility early.

Salary support will depend on the needs of the church planter and the context of ministry. A church planter living in a high-cost area will need additional income in order to live within his ministry context. A church planter with small children may need additional income in order for his spouse to remain at home with the children. Salary support may come from a variety of places.

- *Intentional bi-vocational*—over half of Southern Baptist churches are lead by Bi-vocational ministers. This will continue to be an important part of reaching the many unreached people of North America. There are many advantages to being bi-vocational. As it relates to reaching the unreached in North America being bi-vocational opens doors too many people we simply would not have access to.

- *Missions Organizations*—Organizations like a local association or state convention often contributes to a church planter's salary for a period of time.
- *Sponsoring and partnering churches*—these churches serve as key supporters for church planting. There are some churches that are able to underwrite an entire church planting project, while other times a network of partners can come together to provide funding.
- *Individuals*—In addition to churches, individuals often desire to be a part of a particular church plant in terms of financial support. This most often happens when a relationship is involved.
- *Businesses*—There are a number of growing businesses that desire to give a percentage of their resources directly to some type of missions project. Regardless of where the resources come from, it is the responsibility of the planter to develop and maintain a healthy relationship with his partners. In addition, it is the responsibility of the planter to see that there are adequate resources in place before he sets out on a church planting project.

How will I pay for it?

The vision you write you must underwrite. Better yet, the vision God writes, He can and will underwrite. It is important that a church planter does not give the full charge of raising resources to anyone else. It is ultimately his responsibility and he cannot put blame on anyone else for resources that do not materialize.

People give to people. When it comes to raising resources it is also important to understand that people give to people. Those who are most likely to support your ministry will be those with whom you have had significant relational experiences and your current relationships. Church planters have two primary sources for raising support: churches and his personal relationships with individuals.

Vision Attracts Resources:

Never underestimate the power of vision. People with big resources are usually attracted to people with a big vision. Resources are in the harvest. It is important from day one that you look for resources in the harvest. Developing givers from within the new church is a primary task of the church planter and a basic function of discipleship. People you disciple most often want to turn around and support the work.

First, we need to be constantly bringing our needs before God, expecting Him to provide for them. Secondly, we must develop good skills in providing people the opportunity to invest in the kingdom and inviting them to do so. If you believe what you are doing is of God and is really making a difference, then asking is natural and easy.

People need a reason and opportunity to give. People with resources are always seeking to find a good reason and opportunity to give. They have lived their entire lives making good use of their resources and are looking to invest their resources in credible ways that will make a kingdom impact.

Resources are best raised prior to moving to the field. Avoid presuming that if you go people will give. Many church planters fail due to limited resources or resources that never materialized once they get on the field. Whenever possible see that resources have been raised and partnerships are firm before moving to the new church plant location. The strategy will aid the new church developer in staying focus and prepared for unexpected circumstances down the road.

CHAPTER 5

LAUNCH PUBLICLY YOUR VISION WITH A COMMITTED CORE GROUP

When we follow the history and life of our Savior Jesus Christ, we can model our effort of church planting by His example. As you will note in the Bible, New Testament church believers involved themselves in fellowship daily. The example let us know that a healthy church is one that automatically grows and continues to expand. I believe one of the greatest examples in the Bible is what the NT church was involved in that facilitated their growth. Every day they continued to meet together in the temple courts. They broke bread in their homes and ate together with glad and sincere hearts, praising God and enjoying the favor of all the people. "And the Lord added to their number daily those who were being saved" (Acts 2:46-47).

Church Planting Patterns:

Jesus spent three years building a group of devoted followers before officially starting the New Testament Church. Following His departure from earth in Acts 2, He poured out His Spirit on 120 believers. By the end of that day, 3,000 individuals were added to the church. From that point on, the church took on a very public dimension that focused on the carrying out of the Great Commission. Just as Christ's baptism signified the beginning of His public ministry, this out-pouring of His Spirit signified the public launch of His church.

A brief description of this church gives insight into its structure. In Acts 2, two functional aspects of the first church are clearly demonstrated. First, they met in the temple courts where the preaching of the gospel was central. Second, they continued to meet from house to house where the ongoing needs of the believers were met.

Many new churches follow this same pattern today. They begin with a time of core group development, followed by some type of public launch and then followed by an ongoing small group structure that may or may not meet in homes. The type of new church beginning varies from context to context. In each situation, the church serves as a strategic means for carrying out the Great Commission. In many of today's traditions, the public launch signifies an important step in the birth of a new church. Some would say that once the church has been launched, it has been birthed. To this end the new group must determine how to appropriately move toward becoming a "church."

Definition of Launching of a New Church:

Important to the launching of "a church is a healthy understanding God's plan for the church. Dennis Hampton, a town and country church planter suggests that: A church is a group of people who meet regularly for Bible study, worship and witness, and see themselves as an ongoing fellowship of believers." Just because you have a public launch doesn't necessarily mean you have a church. There is no such thing as an instant church, although a church can be made up of a few believers meeting in a home. The key to the birthing of a new church is the group carrying out the basic biblical functions of the church while seeing itself as a church. This separates a house church from a small group that meets in a home.

Church Planting Approaches:

Because churches take various forms, there is no one way to launch a new church. However, there are two basic start-up strategies that will impact a majority of church models. The first basic start-up strategy involves moving from core to crowd. This approach emphasizes building the core of individuals until it reaches critical mass. When this happens the core usually desires to participate in some form of public worship that may or may not involve a public launch. Once the group begins worshiping together, it will either grow inward or lack a missional impact, or it will utilize existing relational networks for inviting unbelievers into a public worship celebration. While this approach may lack a definite launch event, the public nature of its ministry becomes more apparent.

A second approach moves from crowd to core and has a very clear public launch. This approach may begin with a core group, but in this context the core is mobilized to launch a service where the public is invited to become a part of its fellowship. This approach often includes an aggressive marketing plan targeting the un-churched. It is not uncommon for these churches to attract a large number of un-churched/unsaved people from day one. It is also important to understand that when attracting a large crowd one can anticipate a significant reduction in attendance within two to three weeks. Therefore, if a planter is creating a structure from day one to handle 200 people, then the first service will need to attract approximately 300 to 400 people. In most cases, he can expect 50 percent slide over a period of three to four weeks following the launch service.

Church Planting Models:

There are a number of traditional and nontraditional church planting models that impact the nature of the public launch for the new church. Six models have been identified that represent a majority of churches being planted throughout North America. The traditional church planting models are the program-based model, the purpose-based model, the seeker-based model, and the ministry based model. Nontraditional church planting models are the relation-based model and the affinity-based model.

The distinction between the traditional and the nontraditional church planting models relates primarily to the forms and structures of the new churches. Traditional models tend toward church forms and structures that require buildings, paid staff, et cetera. Nontraditional church planting models are more organic in nature and may meet anywhere. They often have lay pastors and are relationally driven. Below are brief descriptions of each model.

1. Program-based church planting is the planting of a church that will minister to people and grow through a variety of church programs. These programs will consist of some combination of evangelism, discipleship, youth, children's, men, women, and music ministries, missions, and social ministries.
2. Purpose-based church planting is the planting of a church that will focus on the five purposes of a church, which are outreach, worship, fellowship, discipleship, and service.
3. Seeker-based church planting is the planting of churches that intentionally target specific seeker populations and position themselves to respond to their needs. Everything done in the church service focuses on connecting with the spiritual seeker.
4. Ministry-based church planting is the planting of a church that will go into the community, impact people's lives, and draw them toward the gospel. Meeting specific social and spiritual needs of the audience is emphasized.

5. Relation-based church planting is relatively new and attempts to solve the riddle of reaching and congregationalizing people who reject institutional forms of church structure. Relation-based churches are networks of single-cell churches or house churches. These churches are relational and spread along relational lines through natural social networks.
6. Affinity-based church planting involves the starting of a church among a specific people group or population segment. These groups of people are distinguished by ethnicity, language, worldview, socioeconomic factors, and/or lifestyle preferences.

In each of these models, the environment in which the church is planted impacts the launch approach. Churches planted in a multi-housing environment will likely be launched differently than a church in a fast-growing, suburban environment.

Pre-launch Services:

Traditional church planting models usually take on some sort of launch where the new congregation invites the community to participate in regular, weekly worship services. The church planter, planting team, and the core group often will spend from three months to one year in preparation for the public launch.

While some church plants utilize a one-time launch service, others choose to hold pre-launch services. This launch strategy usually includes a worship service or event on a monthly and/or quarterly schedule for three to six months leading up to weekly worship services. This pre-launch strategy is often referred to as a preview service. Preview services give the public an opportunity to preview the worship style prior to the launch. There are a number of advantages to this approach. Some of the advantages include:

- An opportunity for people to experience vision before making a commitment to join the core group.
- An opportunity to test equipment and general flow of the service.
- An opportunity to test the effectiveness of the church planting approach.
- An opportunity to make adjustments prior to weekly services.
- An opportunity to develop existing leaders, while attracting new ones to expand the core group.
- An opportunity to intensify evangelism and discipleship.
- An opportunity to solicit feedback.

A second type of pre-launch service involves conducting some type of outreach or ministry event. This approach must be culturally relevant to the target setting and is an integral part of a church planting strategy that uses the pre-launch method.

Preview and pre-launch services and/or events present opportunities for a core group to give the community a "feel" for the worship style, Christian fellowship, and the general leadership vision of the church planting team. The excitement that is generated during the pre-launch phase will either enhance enthusiasm for the public launch or create a negative attitude toward the new congregation.

Church Plants that Don't Launch:

The "launch" of a house-based church, church of cell groups, and some rural groups may vary. In some cases, these groups may never "invite" the community to come. It is purely relational. Individual core group members cultivate, invite, and bring people. The cultivation is ongoing. There is no rehearsal or formal launch. With cell-based and home-based churches, they are "launched" the first time they meet. This is a key issue with some "relation-based" church starts. Group members invite people with whom they have developed relationships. Their shared vision and the form of leadership that emerges will determine how they express being a church. For some, that will be a decision to "be" and act now as a church, but it may not involve or require a public launch.

- Do you have a shared vision for what the church is to be like?
- Do you have an appropriate meeting place?
- Is your worship team in place?
- Have you communicated to the community a clear understanding of who you are?
- Do you have adequate child care and children's programming?
- Do you have small groups or Bible study groups in place?
- Have you appropriately publicized the launch?
- Are you prepared to carry out the ongoing ministry of the church?
- Do you have an appropriate evangelism strategy in place?

If your approach to planting includes a public launch here are some suggestions:

- Begin simple.
- Evaluate and get feedback.
- Visit a number of churches prior to launching.
- Conduct rehearsal services.
- Add elements only when you are ready.
- Major on your communication style.
- Be relevant.
- Be spiritual.
- Meet people where they are.
- Challenge people to make incremental commitments.
- Celebrate life change.

Regardless, if your church plant includes a public launch or not, it is important that you prepare for the public ministry of the church plant. Failure to do so may result in a new church turning inward and failing to have an impact on the people you felt called to reach.

CHAPTER 6

MOBILIZE AND EVANGELIZE THE UN-CHURCHED

When the planning and structuring process has been completed, reaching out to the community becomes crucial to sustaining the ongoing effort of church planting. As recorded in biblical text, "Then the churches throughout all Judea, Galilee, and Samaria had peace and were edified. And walking in the fear of the Lord and in the comfort of the Holy Spirit, they were multiplied" (Acts 9:31)

Regardless of your strategy or model for planting churches, at some point you will need to be mobilized so that ministry will be multiplied. The very heart of Jesus Great Commission is the call to "make disciples." A believer's experiences and understanding of what it means to be a disciple greatly impacts his or her method or approach for mobilizing and multiplying ministry.

Asking the question, "What does a disciple look and behave like?" can be a good exercise. One's response to this question often depends on his understanding of church. Those who see discipleship through the eyes of a programmatic approach to church might describe a disciple as someone who attends certain worship services throughout the week, gives an offering on Sunday morning, serves on a committee, and participates in the programs of the church. On the other hand, one who sees discipleship from a relational approach (house church or small group church) might describe discipleship in terms of commitment and participation in community.

While there are many ways to describe what it means to be a disciple, Jesus extended three commands that get at the heart of what it means to be a disciple. At the same time, these commands address three basic processes that occur within the organized church following some type of public launch of ministry.

Come and See:

In John 1:39 Jesus invited the first disciples to "come . . . and see." Upon hearing this invitation, we are told that these disciples went and spent a day with Him. Planting a church builds an environment where people can come and see.

In today's context, many of those with little or no Christian memory often begin the discipleship process prior to conversion. They make a decision to convert only after they join community and experience the church as a community.

Within this context it becomes the church planter's responsibility to create an environment where unreached people can "come and see." There are a variety of environments that can be utilized for this type of evangelism: one's home, a small group, a missions opportunity, a social gathering, and/or a worship service.

In church planting, most leaders utilize small groups or a worship service as the consistent environment where relationships and experiences can come together. There are three factors the church planter should be concerned with in establishing an environment that will move people toward relationship and experience.

These factors are the attraction, pace, and grace factors.

- *Attraction Factor*: The attraction factor relates to creating environments that encourage ongoing participation. Regardless of what kind of environment one is creating, unreached people are most often looking for authenticity and relevance. If you can gain their trust and you meet a need, they are most likely to make the next step. A simple sermon series on real life issues dealt with in an honest way does much to creating this kind of environment.

- *Pace Factor*: Through the years, you may or may not have been involved in planting churches but may have noticed that there is a direct correlation between the endurance of one's commitment and the time taken to make that commitment. Creating an environment where people are not rushed or pushed to make the next step, but where they are allowed to come at their own pace, results in long-term discipleship. Jesus allowed the disciples to progress at their own pace, which for the most part appears to have taken about three years.

- *Grace Factor*: We shouldn't expect unbelievers to act like believers before they are believers. It is human nature to long for acceptance. Creating an accepting, grace-filled environment will give many unreached people what they need to continue the journey. Jesus had no tolerance for the self-righteous. The example of how He dealt with the woman caught in the very act of adultery in John 8:1-11 is a perfect example of grace.

In this kind of environment, people tend to assimilate around a number of activities and relationships. The following examples represent natural opportunities where unreached people can "come and see."

1. The table is an excellent place to engage people. A simple study of the life of Jesus demonstrates that the table played an important role in His relationships.

    Everywhere He went He sat down at a table with others and "broke bread. "On a practical level, many new churches do a good job of utilizing their hospitality ministries in moving people toward a deeper commitment. It can be something as

simple as a cup of coffee and a donut before or after a worship service, a cookout for the entire church, or one-on-one meals at a local restaurant. Food has a way of breaking down barriers and is a proven means for creating intimacy in most cultures.
2. Small groups are another proven way of engaging people. Once someone decides to participate in some type of small group setting, the likelihood of them dropping out decreases significantly. Church planters must be wise in providing a variety of small group opportunities that are attractive to unreached people.
3. Ministry and task are key for moving people toward a healthy commitment.

    In a new church setting, there are many tasks that can be performed by nonbelievers.

    When this happens, individuals are validated and tend to move forward on their journey toward authentic discipleship.
4. Information can prove to be invaluable in the process of moving people toward discipleship. Helping unreached people understand what it means to be a disciple in simple and organic terms is essential. In addition, communicating the vision, mission, and values of the church as it relates to your commitment to making disciples is crucial. Many existing and new churches utilize some type of newcomer orientation and life development process for accomplishing this.

Follow Me:

While "come and see" focuses on encouraging those who are searching, the command to "Follow Me" (found in Mark 1:17) encourages those who are deciding to become fully devoted followers of Christ. Once again, a major obstacle to following Jesus is a simple understanding of what it means to be a disciple. Most of us make it far too complicated.

What does it mean to be a devoted follower of Jesus? Let me suggest four simple behaviors.

1. *Live like Jesus lived.*—while many people today are turned off to the church, few are turned off to Jesus. Teaching and preaching through the life of Jesus is a must in a new church. Texts like the "Sermon on the Mount" take on a new relevance as unreached people discern whether or not Christianity is for them. Just what does it mean to live like Jesus lived? Perhaps the best Scripture for understanding this statement is found in Philippians 2:5-8:

   "Your attitude should be the same as that of Christ Jesus: Who, being in very nature God, did not consider equality with God something to be grasped, but made himself nothing, taking the very nature of a servant, being made in human likeness. And being found in appearance as a man, he humbled himself and became obedient to death—even death on a cross!"

   The single characteristic that describes Jesus is His willingness to decrease Himself even to the extent of death. His motivation was His commitment to the will of the Father. Living like Jesus lived is a daily surrender to the character and calling of Jesus. As John the Baptist suggested, "I must decrease in order that He might increase."

2. *Love like Jesus loved.*—the life of Jesus is told through a collection of stories and pictures we call the gospels. These stories and pictures give us a vivid accounting of how Jesus loved. His death on the cross demonstrates the extent of His Love. To love like Jesus loved can be seen clearly in His relationship with His disciples, His commitment to Mary and Martha, His devotion to His own mother, His grace demonstrated to the woman caught in the very act of adultery, His tears for

Jerusalem, His friendship with "sinners," and His forgiveness to His executioners. Loving like Jesus loved is a lifelong quest of extending His love to those around us in practical ways.

3. *Lead like Jesus led.*—Jesus is the greatest leader of all time. He spent His life with a specific mission, but in the process of fulfilling that mission He poured Himself extensively into the lives of 12 individuals, while maintaining various levels of influence over many more. In return, those into whom He poured His life multiplied themselves into the lives of many others. If one follows carefully the leadership of Jesus throughout the gospels a pattern evolves. This pattern consists of the following process:

   - *He mobilized*—He invited people to enter into community with Him.
   - *He modeled*—He lived His life of love in the context of this community.
   - *He mentored*—He sent those in community with Him out to "do likewise."
     This was most often accompanied by a time of debriefing.
   - *He multiplied*—He ultimately left them in charge of His mission as He returned to the Father.

4. *Leave what Jesus left behind.*—Ultimately, a disciple leaves what Jesus left behind, which is people who live like He lived, love like He loved, and lead like He led. The true mark of a disciple is that they leave a legacy of other disciples who are represented in future generations.

The life of Jesus demonstrates what it means to make disciples from a very organic perspective. A danger we face in program discipleship is that it becomes more about what you do than what you become. When

Henry Blackaby was asked about the disciplines involved in discipleship, "he suggested that the problem with talking about them is we begin to focus on the disciplines when Christianity is about a relationship. This is the danger in setting up organizational processes within the church. Priority should always be placed on the process and not the procedure. Once a clear understanding of this happens, the new church can create environments and processes for facilitating a maturing relationship." An example of an organizational process developed for encouraging a growing relationship among believers within the framework of a church is the baseball diamond that Rick Warren uses to mobilize disciples at Saddleback Church. A key question to answer is how will you encourage the development of disciples within your context? What processes will you put in place to serve their needs for development?

Go and Make Disciples:

Jesus' final words to His disciples were related to multiplication. In Matthew 28:19-20, He said, "Therefore go and make disciples of all nations, baptizing them in the name of the Father and of the Son and of the Holy Spirit, and teaching them to obey everything I have commanded you. And surely I am with you always, to the very end of the age."

Multiplying your influence as a disciple is the very essence of the Great Commission. God has chosen to use the planting of His church among every unreached people to spread this influence. Multiplication is a mind-set, as well as a commitment. It begins with the under-standing that we are called to be and make disciples. Therefore, multiplication must be part of the DNA that runs through the church planter and the new church. When it does, one can see multiplication at work at every level. When multiplication is part of the very fabric that drives the new church, you see the multiplication in every aspect of the church. It is reflected by believers, small groups, ministry, and churches being multiplied.

Inherent to multiplication is our understanding of church. If we see church only as a large organization with paid staff, large buildings, and extensive programming then multiplication is going to be very difficult. At best, we can expect addition. However, if we see church in a more organic form and are willing to plant it in its most transferable form then multiplication can be sure from day one.

When it comes to multiplication, it is essential that we have a biblical understanding of a number of areas:

- *Discipleship*—At the risk of sounding redundant, in order to multiply disciples we must understand the very nature of a healthy disciple. As mentioned earlier, this is one reason Henry Blackaby refused to define it in terms of disciplines.

    This is also the reason we choose to define discipleship in very simple organic terms such as living like Jesus lived, loving like Jesus loved, leading like Jesus led, and leaving behind what Jesus left behind.
- *Community*—when we come to Christ He invites us into community with other disciples. This community often takes the form of some type of small group ministry and structure. The challenge we face in facilitating community is setting it up in a way that encourages multiplication. This requires a high degree of trust and a willingness to relinquish control. In addition, there has to be a large amount of modeling and mentoring in order for effective multiplication to take place. Lastly, one also must be willing to let others fail in order to multiply community.
- *Leaders*—A church planter made the comment that it is our job to qualify the unqualified. The key to multiplying community and churches is multiplying leaders. From day one, this is the challenge in a church plant. Every church planter needs to be strategic in pouring his life into a handful of potential leaders.

Once he has identified this group he can begin giving ministry away to them as they develop. His ultimate objective is to work himself out of a job through the multiplication of these leaders.
- *Churches*—In an environment where disciples, communities, and leaders are multiplied, church multiplication is possible.

The three important components that is crucial in facilitating church growth. These components are assimilating believers, mobilizing disciples, and multiplying the church. Jesus' command to "come and see" gives us key insight into the need for developing environments for providing a safe place for those searching to experience a loving gospel. His command to "follow me" calls us to a lifestyle of discipleship that focuses on life change. And finally, His command to "go make disciples" calls us to multiply our influence at every level. The following chapter is filled with several examples and strategies of growing new church starts.

CHAPTER 7

STRATEGIES FOR GROWING AND SUSTAINING A NEW CHURCH PLANT

Once the launch of the new church process has taken place and the new church plant or mission has become an officially established entity, strategies for growing the new ministry becomes very necessary. The recommendations below will be of utmost importance in sustaining and growing the new church. The recommendations will explore proactive ways of developing and maintaining a consistent growth pattern within your new ministry. An important note to be considered in implementing outreach strategies is the need for committed individuals to assist in carrying out each part of the strategic plan for church growth.

I have experienced down through the years that serving the needs of the community can consistently add value, longevity and stable growth to any congregation within the community. I invite you to consider the simplistic tools below as a way of seeking to establish the church as a part of a community. Each new ministry will be an opportunity for every age group to participate. Strategies and recommendations are as follows:

Recommendations and Considerations:

On average, churches retain 16% of their first-time guests. For example, if your church has a retention rate of 15%, and you attract 2 guests per month (or 24 guests per year), then you only add four new members every year. This is very common pattern among churches . . . . They are very good at keeping people once they come, but they just don't attract enough guests each month to see much growth. But, if this example church were able to attract one guest per week, it could add eight new members each year. Make that two per week, and it could add 16 new members!

Prepare to Receive Guests:

Just like you clean up the house when you are expecting a visitor, you must also do "house cleaning" in the church to prepare it for guests.

Create a Welcoming Atmosphere:

Is your church good at welcoming new people? If not, then it is doubtful many new people will be attracted to your church. Begin by teaching a series of lessons on "hospitality." Create a profile of the average unchurched man and woman who might attend your church and share it with the congregation. Start a task force to plan better ways to welcome new people.

Seek Ways to Develop Healthy Morale:

The main way guests come to a church is through the invitation of present church attendees. However, if your congregation has low morale, people will not invite others to attend. Begin by celebrating positive aspects of your church's ministry. Find ways to interview new people from the pulpit. Ask people whose lives have been touched by your church to share their story. Set some reachable goals and praise the congregation when they are reached.

Be an Advocate for Strong Fellowship:

Some people attend churches without making any friends. If people in your church do not fellowship with each other, it will be difficult to get them to reach out in fellowship with strangers. Begin by hosting bi-monthly church dinners. Sign up people to share meals with each other on a rotating basis. Schedule a half hour fellowship time between Sunday school and your worship service.

Be Creative in Developing Your Church's Welcome:

Most churches perceive themselves as friendly. However, if newcomers don't echo the same sentiment, then you need to improve your welcome. Begin by using ushers, parking attendants, and greeters who are friendly people. Build an information center, where it is easy for new people to ask questions.

Develop your church's plan: Growing churches usually average 4-5% of weekly worship attendees as guests, and eventually retain 20-30% of them as members. Begin by looking over your records for the past one or two years and determine your percentages. If they are as high as those above, rejoice. If not, set a goal to improve your percentages within the next year.

Now that you are prepared for your guests, here are five basic ways you will be successful at attracting new people to your church:

Encourage Word of Mouth Invitations:

Word of mouth is the best way to attract guests to a church. When satisfied people give testimony to others that your church is a great place to attend, you will have all the guests you need. Here's how to encourage word of mouth. Print a general church business card and give everyone in your church 52 cards. Ask them to hand out one each week, along with an invitation to attend your church. Remember, one fourth of non-churched people say they have never been invited to church!

Reward people who bring others:

Just like you thank the cooks after a church dinner, you must also reward church members for bringing guests. Here's one way to do it: When guests register their attendance, provide a place for them to note who invited them. Keep track of people who invite others, and then host an appreciation dessert once each quarter to honor these key people.

Advertise your Church's Ministry:

If your church is small, just getting off the plateau, or located in a place with low visibility, you need to do something to make your church known to potential guests.

Here's one way to advertise: Develop a "first impression piece" about your church. This year, mail it to everyone within a five minute drive of your church. Next year, mail it to everyone within a ten minute drive. The third year, mail it to everyone within a 15 minute drive.

Help Visitors to Feel Welcome but not Uncomfortable:

Growing churches usually have at least three non-threatening entry points. Why? New people find it uncomfortable to attend a church. Here's how to develop low threat entry points: Ask your regular attendees to list the names of un-churched friends. Then have them list things their friends are interested in, such as sports, classes, crafts, etc. Group the various interests together, select the three largest groupings, and then create three new ministries around those three interests this next year.

Welcome guests to church:

When guests come to church, they like to be noticed but feel anonymous. If guests feel in any way embarrassed, they won't come back. Here's one way to welcome guests: Ask regular attendees not to talk with their friends or do any church business but to welcome guests during the first five minutes following your worship service. As soon as you finish your benediction or last song, tell people to "remember the five minute rule."

Embracing Ministry Opportunities by Developing Service Ministries:

I believe very strongly in the power of serving the community to impact the church growth. Serving isn't some trick to create growth, or some way to tie God's hands and force Him to grow your church, serving is a way to treat people the way God wants to see them treated, and it's the very essence of God's personality. That's why it's so powerful. Of course, the hardest part of serving is figuring out what to do and who will assist you. You will experience individuals coming to your church location just to see what they can get but over time your consistent effort will draw those whom God intended to be a part of your ministry. Listed below you will find ways to serve your community.

A Free Store:

The idea is that you collect new and gently used clothes, or really anything else you want to include, from your church members and from donations from the community. Then, once a month or so, depending on your supply, go to a poor neighborhood and allow people to come in and select a set number of items. There's no charge for the items, but people can only get so many per person or maybe give out bags at the entrance and each person can only take what they can fit in the bag.

Also, remember to contact local stores and ask if they have any donations. Or, better yet, local clothing manufacturers. Many factories end up with clothing that isn't good enough to sell, but is still perfectly good, it's just damaged in some way. Just be warned that some donated items will be ready for the trash heap when they arrive, so plan in advance how to politely decline or dispose of those items. It is possible to get rid of them without hurting people's feelings, so long as you plan ahead and figure out the best way to handle those cases. And, I would suggest disposing of poor quality items rather than just hoping they get taken fast. You want a reputation for amazing service and love, not as a place to get stuff no one will ever wear.

Serving the Elderly and Ill:

Offer your service to the elderly; maybe they would want someone to drive them to see the doctor. People don't have any way of knowing for real if you're from a church or not. We should remember that in serving the community, especially the elderly, you must win confidence. Preparing lunches is one way to help families within the community to help look out for their family members. Working with this population requires special care, since you have to prove your reliability to those you seek to help. That's why the best route is to contact places that might know of people interested in your church's help, such as doctor's offices, physical therapy clinics, maybe a grocery store in a part of town where a lot of elderly people live, etc. There are plenty of people that have trouble running errands, or who need so much help that they wear their friends and family out with driving them around (just imagine what it would do to your work schedule if your spouse had to get chemo every week and you had to take them, or if your sister couldn't drive because she lost their leg in a car crash but she still needed groceries and her kids still needed to get to soccer practice). So, find areas where people like that would pass by and tell the doctors or staff working there that you would love to help and that they should feel free to give out the contact information to the church to anyone interested in scheduling a ride somewhere. That way, the doctor or the manager of the store will get to know you and can vouch for you as a safe person to rely on. Plus, they'll also have a better idea of those who really need the help. Finding older church members who are not working is a good way to facilitate involvement in the church ministry efforts.

Bring Gift Baskets to the Police and Firefighters of Your City:

Tons of people go feed the homeless on Thanksgiving or send thank you cards to military personnel stationed overseas who are away from loved ones, but few people remember that there are police officers who are working and risking their life while their child is having their first Christmas. When you bring them gift baskets or candy to share around the office, it means a lot. Of course, before you do this, it would be a good idea to call ahead and make sure you'll come at a convenient time and find out about any rules that govern how you can serve. As government employees, police and firefighters may not be able to accept certain things as gifts, but I'm sure there's something you can do that will meet them where they are.

Look for People that No One Ever Thinks about Serving:

A good example of this would be that for Christmas for the past two years my church went to give gift baskets to the nursing home. Naturally, everyone is eager to do something for the kids and their family, especially during the holidays. It touched the hearts of people because they never expected to be remembered and even doing something small for them really had a huge impact. Other people that are often overlooked would be: trash collectors, case workers for child protective services or welfare, employees of a store (can you think of the last time someone stopped by Target and gave the workers a gift). You can find forgotten people everywhere.

Meet to Pray for Others:

This could be meeting to pray for those in a particular ward of the hospital, or maybe meeting to ask God to show mercy to those with a court date that today, or really any form of interceding for another person's needs. This may not give a lot of publicity, but God wants to see the sick healed and sinners forgiven, so when you line your heart up with His and ask Him to do the things He wants to see happen anyway, your church will move forward, and the community will be changed.

Sack Lunches for Day Laborers:

Depending on where you live, sometimes day laborers will congregate in various areas waiting for people to come by and hire them. If that is common in your city (and it probably is if you live in a medium or large city, you just have to find where), consider packing sack lunches for them and then going out that morning before the laborers get hired and giving them all a lunch to take with them.

Think of What You Would Do if it were Christmas, and Do Those Things When It's not:

This is a great source of ideas for serving. It's amazing how many cool service ideas people come up with around the holidays, and most of them would be even more meaningful if you did them when serving wasn't a fashionable thing, like it is during holidays. It could be something as simple as making more of a conscious effort to smile at others (which we all try to do around Christmas, even when we are angry over the mall parking), or feeding the homeless, or donating gifts to the less fortunate (there are birthdays to consider, after all).

Creating Ministries of Helps to the Community:

Do you have several teachers in your church? Set up tutoring once a week. Do you have nurses? Ask a store if you can set up a table where people can get advice on dieting issues. Do you have college students? Call local high schools and offer to come in once a month so juniors and seniors can ask questions about the college application process.

Collect School Supplies to Donate to Local Schools:

Collecting school supplies is a great way to serve because even the smallest gesture seems huge to the recipient. Trust me, I teach a few nights a week and you'd be amazed how many problems come up. Most are trivial, but, over time, they wear teachers down and make them feel unappreciated. If you do something even as simple as befriend one teacher, you'll touch them deeply and other teachers will also take notice.

Serve the Unemployed / Under-employed:

There are always persons who are unemployed within the community. Use this opportunity to offer your service to people in need. Help them polish their résumé, look for jobs, etc. You can also help people with the paperwork needed to apply for unemployment and other government assistance. Create a job bank or resource center and notify the community that you are willing to assist them. It is one sure way of drawing new persons to your church and ministry.

Water Give A-ways:

These are pretty simple, but fun. Get a group together, use bottled water, and find an intersection with a median you can stand on and be out of the way of traffic. Then, just hold up a sign saying "Free Water."

It helps if your team dresses alike (same t-shirt or something) so the event feels more planned and people will be more comfortable. Also, I would suggest you pick an intersection that is neither deserted, nor flooded with cars, because if the intersection is too busy you won't have time to give out the water to everyone who wants it and that tends to encourage you to take risks and some cars will wait for you and cause a traffic jam, etc.

Stage Plays, Talent Shows, etc. at Local Nursing Homes:

This is also a great way to engage your youth, by letting those who are interested in drama have fun with the shows, while also reaching out and serving those in the nursing home.

Sports Programs for Youth:

Develop sports with seasonal activities such as basketball, skating events, field trips, youth events that will attract young people. Out of the activities recruit volunteers to help with tutoring, and mentoring support. Every community suffers from lack of fathers and family support. Use the above opportunities to recruit supporters who will join you in your evangelistic campaign.

Sharing your Mission Statement and Vision with Leaders in the Community:

Meet with the Mayor of your City and share with him your vision for your church. Ask for help from other City leaders on how your church may impact the community in a positive way? Go and visit such businesses as barber shops and convenient stores, they will become points of contact to promote your church. As I was sharing my vision with the mayor of our city; he gave me information about a government grant to support the elderly in a low income housing project. In six months we were successful in obtaining an award for the facility. The blessing came about through sharing the vision and mission statement of our church.

Vacation Bible School in the Park:

In past years I have used vacation Bible School as a summer camp. Conducting a summer camp/vocational bible school in the park is a great outreach tool to reach out to youth who cannot afford to attend a summer camp. By taking advantage of food programs and swimming pools for the summer and schools who serve free lunches to children during the summer months, you can reduce the financial overhead that will be experienced. Creating low cost ministry opportunities can be a positive way to economically and socially impact the community in which you will serve.

Lock-ins for Youth:

Planning a "Lock In" event can be used to draw youth to your church and provide a platform to address home and family issues. By inviting leaders within the community to be motivational speakers such as police officers, and pastors, young children lives could be positively impacted by learning the importance of good citizenship and receive the benefits of being exposed to positive role models.

Social Media: Ways of reaching out to others:

I believe that as we move into new areas of evangelism the churches must take advantage of present technology in reaching out to others. We must move beyond the traditional aspects to evangelism and go where people are even if it is on the internet. Seriously, I don't see how a church can expect to meet new people without a website. The majority of people these days will check out a church's website before they ever visit the church. If there is no website then there is no visit. I'm not sure I can answer that question of social media for every church. The best effort will be to try to guide leaders towards a decision that's right for their church.

Do you want to reach Younger People?

If you want to reach people these days, you have to go where they are at and younger people hang out in a world of social media. The number one way people under 40 reach me is with a facebook message. Twitter is growing. Email is still common, but not growing at the rate of the other two. For a business to not have anyone responding to their social media streams is equivalent not to answering the phone. You can't simply have a social media presence and expect results. You have to commit to it and work it. Not being active in social media may be worse than not doing it at all.

Can You Afford Not To?

It is important to seek every avenue in reaching people with the Gospel message. Again, I can't answer that question, but can you reach the un-churched people you are attempting to reach without social media? If you can, perhaps you don't need it. If you're not sure, perhaps you should give it a try. One suggestion I have is to find the person or persons in your church who are already active in social media. Get them to volunteer to help the church in this area. You don't have to assign this to a staff person who isn't interested or doesn't understand. Find the right person, give them authority and responsibility, and let them help build the Kingdom through your church and social media.

Finance your Vision Through Faith-based Economic & Community Development Revenue:

There are creative avenues for assisting religious organizations in financing their visions. The approach is (Holistic) which considers the whole person. Usually, churches view themselves as going against the grain when they move outside of the box and began to explore areas of touching people in untraditional ways. Below are recommendations for Generating Revenue for Christian Faith-Based Economic & Community Organizations which are alternative to funding your "Kingdom Vision"

Components of Economic & Community Development Ministry:

The Income Producing Services—Economic & Community Development Corporation (CDC/ECD) (501c3) (Grant Funding)

- Utilize Real Estate Developments to completely cover the expenses associated with your vision
- Implement techniques to purchase property with no money down & bad credit
- Improve the credit rating of the ministry or non-profit you serve
- Analyze your resources, the seller and the property
- Acquire foreclosure properties at the courthouse auctions each month using partners or existing cash
- Identify and negotiate successful land and commercial property investments
- Owner finance property for quick sales and cash out for your ministry, school, or non-profit
- Find financially secure people to create partnerships to invest in real estate
- Acquire the right residential and/or commercial property with your available resources

- Write offers to purchase property and get the property closed with the title company
- Each of the above recommendations lead to what I call is a process call "Creative Financing" or "Alternative Financing" There are ways to carry out your vision if you have the faith to take risks. God will bless us with what we need to do His work. I am a personal witness that our efforts will be blessed if we take a walk of faith.

Community Development Financial Institution—(CDFI Credit Union)

- Venture Capital to Start-up or expand existing businesses in Low Income Areas
- Mortgage Financing to Low-Income First Time Homebuyers
- Commercial and Mixed-Use Financing
- Real Estate Non-Profit Developers
- Business Financing Training
- Permanent Financing
- Short Term Debt
- Creative Financing
- Teach those whom you serve to take advantage of financial opportunities.

Retail Business Incubator Program (RBIP)

- Retail Business Incubator Program is designed to provide one-stop shop needs of the community—Provide entrepreneurs with the expertise, networks, and tools they need to succeed
- Entrepreneurial Training, Business Development and Technical Assistance
- Career Counseling, Job Placement, and On-The-Job Training
- Real Estate Business Space for Existing and Start-up Businesses

Young Adult Community Residential Services

- Individual, Group, and Family Counseling
- Household Management Skills Training
- Problem Solving/Conflict Strategies
- Anger Management Training
- Substance Abuse Counseling
- Money Management Training
- Communication Skill Building
- Employment Skills Training
- Foods programs-feeding youth during the summer while providing educational activities.

Vehicle Donation Program-donated from State of Government Agencies

- Develop vehicle donation program
- Procedures for disposing donated vehicles
- Determine selling price of donated vehicles
- Determine market value of donated vehicle
- Storage of donated vehicles
- Maintain and repair donated vehicles

The list of possibilities goes on and on. By using legal ways you can reach out to people who you would otherwise be incapable of providing services to. Jesus said, "when you have done so unto the least of my brethren ye have done it unto me" By utilizing the opportunity God has given us we can position ourselves in the place to be a greater positive impact to our communities and fulfilling the "Great Commission"

Radio and Television Ministry:

There is no denying that Christian programming can provide inspiration and encouragement. It can help launch your ministry to new levels, but it is no substitute for the God-ordained interaction and unity of a body of believers. Though the viewer may warm to the personality of the television preacher, the two-way interaction of believers ministering to each other is missing. Sinners have been brought to a salvation experience through Christian television and Radio Broadcasts, but to grow in sanctification and Christlikeness, each believer needs the accountability and watchful care that comes only through face-to-face relationship with another believer who can personally love and share joys and sorrows.

Community and Relationships in Church Growth:

I believe as we seek more proactive ways of establishing God's church within the community, there is a need to consider relationship building. The question is should churches seek a more active role in developing relationship to sustain their church organization? First the church must become a stronger community itself. These comments really made me stop and think as it raises issues I have assumed rather than looked at it in depth. To address these issues let me start with a quick summary of the church growth modeling work.

The main claim of the limited enthusiasm model is that conversion growth is driven by a subset of the church, who I call enthusiasts, who do not remain enthusiastic in their recruitment indefinitely. This conversion growth depends on contact between the enthusiasts and the unbelievers in the community. This loss of effectiveness can be for spiritual reasons, but more often than not it is that their enthusiasm gets more and more directed towards the church and they lose their contacts in the wider community. I believe this mind set will eventually hinder any church effort to expand.

The amount of growth that comes through the enthusiasts, and how long that growth lasts, depends on their effectiveness in reproducing themselves, either from new converts, or from existing Christians. However, additionally, the growth also comes from the amount of the unbelieving community they are in contact with. If either their effectiveness or their community contact is reduced, the growth will be less, and cease quicker. Because of the increased effort needed as the unbelieving pool gets smaller, growth ceases before all the unbelievers are converted.

Of course there will be church growth through the children of believers becoming believers themselves. At one time this kept the church sustainable regardless of conversions, but not these days of worldly distractions there must be a constant proactive effort to avoid the trap of lack of motivation. There were times in the past where churches could be successfully large even though they had little success in mission. In today's religious environment, our strategies must change to combat secular competing with evangelistic and mission efforts.

Also for the local congregation there will be transfer growth as Christians move into the community, and some Christians choose to change churches. For churches on growing housing estates, and churches with growing reputations, transfers can be the main source of growth, giving success for the church as a "service organization" with little success in seeing the world converted!

One of the biggest mistakes a church can make is to assume it has effective contact with all the unbelievers in its community. Evangelistic efforts should include ways of continuing to seek out those who may not know Christ. I suspect in many cases the church only has any serious contact with a minority of its wider community. In that case conversion growth is going to be much harder. So a conclusion of the limited enthusiasm theory is that a church must work on building effective links with the community in order to make conversion growth easier to achieve.

Those who lead evangelistic efforts within the church must realize is the massive difference it might make to their conversion growth if they only increase their contact with the community by a small amount. If the community they are in contact with is increased by 10%, then that has the same effect as increasing the effectiveness of the enthusiasts by 10%. However that can have a disproportionate effect on growth.

If the enthusiasts' effectiveness is a long way from the revival growth threshold then a 10% increase would make little difference to the church's growth. However if it were near the revival growth threshold, such a small increase could easily double church growth over the long term. This is a case of small things can make a big difference.

The same argument applies if the enthusiasts are to reproduce themselves out of existing church members. There needs to be a strong spiritual community among the church, rather than a loose collection of individuals, or church of largely non-overlapping interest groups.

Thus there is a need for a church to be an integral part of the community it is contained within, and to be a strong community itself. The former is a big challenge in modern life where people's community is often their work place, rather than their geographical location. The latter is a big challenge where church life is driven more by personal preference, i.e. consumer demand, rather than an army under central orders.

Of course people will always say "the Holy Spirit can override all of this, all we need is revival." True. But generally speaking people respond to the good news because they hear it from someone who is sent. That implies a contact between communities not just enthusiasm on the part of the Christian. We can be as on fire for God as it is possible to be, but if we don't have real contact with fellow believers and unbelievers the fire of the Spirit is not passed on. Such a scenario is about as alien one can get to New Testament thinking, which is all about building quality churches and going into the world.

Likewise it is not enough to have contact with the community if there is not a real fire of the Holy Spirit in the enthusiasts of the church. They must have something worth passing on. In the current debate between the emerging church approach and the approach of those who seek revival it is easy to be so caught up with the need of the Holy Spirit that we forget to have contact with the community. There has to be something worth passing on, serving others, as noble as it is, is not enough. Unbelievers can do that. Believers have to have something specific to Christianity to pass on, the power of God to change lives through faith in Christ.

Programmatic Strategies for Pastoral Leaders:

In spite of the huge ministries and churches we see on television, the majority of churches in the United States have fewer than one hundred members. The following tips apply to really small, struggling churches, as well as average size churches that have reached a plateau. Pasturing small churches can be a challenge, but there are a few simple things you can do to help your church grow. The following suggestions will be helpful in structuring the small church for growth. I have practiced the strategies below while structuring the church for growth.

Be Passionate:

If pastors are going to grow their church, they must be passionate about the ministry. Those in the Bible who accomplished great things were passionate and committed men and women. Elijah was passionate and unafraid when he confronted Ahab, the king (1 Kings 17-19). As a result, he saw a nation touched by God's power. Let's be passionate men and women of God. Our ministry will be the better for it.

Become a servant of Prayer:

We must be men and women of prayer. No great work has ever been accomplished for God outside of much time in earnest prayer. It was said of Jesus, "And in the morning, rising up a great while before day, he went out, and departed into a solitary place, and there prayed" (Mark 1:35 KJV). It was also said of the early church, "These all with one mind were continually devoting themselves to prayer along with the women" (Acts 1:14 KJV).

According to the late Dr. Paul E. Paino, frequently said, "Great preaching and great praying alone will not build great churches." Some of the greatest preachers and most committed prayer warriors continue to pastor small struggling churches. It takes more. God may move and bring us people, but it's up to us to keep them.

Structure the Church For Growth:

You can pray and God may bring people into your church but if you don't structure for growth you will never keep them. Much of a pastor's time should be devoted to praying on how the Holy Spirit would have him structure and restructure the church. We must constantly structure and restructure to allow for continued growth and to maintain growth that has taken place. You must change the way your church is structured at every level or plateau of growth you experience. This is one of the reasons God has placed you where you are. Paul told Titus, "For this reason I left you in Crete, that you should set in order the things that are lacking" (Titus 1:5 KJV).

You should constantly be in prayer about how you may need to structure and restructure the classes (Sunday school and/or children's church) in your church your ministry grows; this will need to take place in order to maintain the growth God brings your way. This needs to takes place at every level or plateau of growth you experience. You should also be constantly praying and brain storming on how you should set in order every aspect of the church.

This includes your leadership (elders and deacons) and who is put in charge of different areas and responsibilities of ministry. All things in the church must be subject to change as the need arises. Frequently, trouble comes our way to force us to change and restructure the church as is seen in Acts 6:1-7. New structure and delegated responsibility allowed for continued growth in the New Testament church. It also allowed for pressure to be alleviated from the Apostles (or you as pastor) and allowed them to prioritize their ministry.

Prayerfully Choose Proper Meeting Places:

Make sure your facilities and meeting places are up to par. No matter what type of building you have, make sure it looks the best it possibly can. Paint and cleaning supplies do wonders for both the inside and outside—and always keep up on the grounds. People's first impression of your facility will make all the difference in the world. It may very well determine whether they come back the second time or not.

Be Creative in Your Advertising Campaign:

Use media and publications in your area to let others know about your ministry. Almost all towns and cities have some sort of news outlets that offer free public service announcements and news releases. It's foolish not to take advantage of them.

When pasturing I've always used local news outlets for nearly everything we had going on. Even if it's as small as a pitch-in dinner, vocational bible school, a special meeting, or a concert; let people know about it. Write up some general information, explain your event or activity thoroughly, and then take it to the local paper. You can also mail a condensed version of the announcement to your local Christian radio or TV stations. If promoting a concert or guest speaker, always submit a picture with your news release. They will usually include a small photo if they have room, and a picture will help bring attention to your advertising.

Be Intentional in Developing Signs and Church Information:

Make sure your signs and displays are clear and accurate. For example, make sure Sunday school and service times are clearly listed, especially if you have multiple services. If service times are not accurate, it can be very confusing to guests and newcomers. Also, make sure relevant information is kept up-to-date on marquis, Internet advertisements (denominational information if it applies), websites, brochures, letterhead, business cards, and other ministry materials.

Be a good Example of Accessibility:

Pastors, we must be accessible. Make sure your contact information is displayed clearly so people can reach you. Preferably, you should hold regular office hours so people will know how and when to reach you at the church—so they won't have to call you at home (unless it's an emergency). If you are bi-vocational, or live a distance from the church, make sure you have a local number where you can be reached. The church should at least provide a cell phone with a local number for their pastor. For a few years, I pastor a church that is a half hour away from my home. At times you may be necessary to forward the church phone to your home.

You may be small but Think and act Big:

The Bible says, "so as a man thinketh in his heart, so is he" (Proverbs 23:7). If you are going to grow your church, you must think and act as if it is larger than it is.

Be Consistent in Whatever You Do:

If you have certain time schedules for your services, make sure you keep them. It is my belief that you should never cancel a service for fear that someone who has been thinking about checking out your church. Be a god steward by keeping the doors open because someone may come for a visit and find you were not there. The church doors should always be open to receive those that God will send our way.

Be an Example of Punctuality:

If you tell someone you are going to meet them at such and such a time—be there when you said you would. If you have meetings listed or advertised at a certain time, you must start at those times. Frequently, people get in the habit of arriving late to church. If they arrive late and find the service has already started, it will teach them to be on time. On the other hand, if visitors come at a certain time because it is advertised as such, only to find that the service is delayed, they will not be punctual the next time (if they come back at all).

Lead Your Congregation to Pursue Excellence:

Paul wrote, "That ye may approve things that are excellent" (Philippians 1:10). We must be the best we can in all that we do. We must be professional in appearance, the best we can be at preaching and teaching, how we order and conduct the service, the worship, etc. Think of what you have seen when attending a small church as compared to what you see when visiting a large church. You wouldn't expect to visit a large church and see the order of service, worship, timeliness or so on conducted in a haphazard manner would you? Of course you wouldn't. If a small church expects to grow it should do no less.

Always Appreciate Visitors:

Visitors are very important to the growth of your church. For each visitor, make sure you conduct the following:

Welcome Guests:

It's important for all visitors to feel welcomed, cared for, and accepted (Romans 15:7), but not embarrassed. Visitors should never be put on the spot or feel like they are on display.

Get Visitor's Contact Information:

Make sure you fill out a card or sheet with each visitor's basic contact information. What is normally used is a visitor's card requesting information such as name, mailing address, phone number (home and cell), and email address.

Contact them:

It's imperative that visitors be contacted. A letter should be sent to them first thing Monday morning thanking them for visiting your church. If the pastor doesn't have time, someone should be designated to send the letter out for him (in his name). By the end of the week, the visitor should be contacted by phone as well. I usually waited until Thursday so they had time to receive the letter I sent earlier in the week. If they are open, a home visit can be good.

Visitation and Follow Up:

The sheep or congregation need to be visited and followed up on as well. If a member of the congregation misses two or three weeks in a row, they should be called or visited. We never know what they may be going through. Jesus stressed the importance of this in Luke 15 with three illustrations: the lost sheep, coin and son.

I would rather have people complain because we loved them too much than because no one ever called them when they left. If someone leaves to attend another church, you should let them go. If they have strayed from the body, we must go after them.

Regular visitation is needed as well. A phone call doesn't take that much time. Set apart a regular time to call people to see how they are doing, pray with them, and show them you care. You'll be amazed by the results. As the church grows, this can also be delegated to the leadership.

I also usually called everyone on our mailing list for special events and services we were having. I would go through our entire mailing list of everyone who had ever visited the church and remind them of what was going on and secure their commitment to be in attendance. As a result, we usually had a good turnout and the people were encouraged. A good turnout to a special service always helps strengthen and encourage the body.

Special Events:

Have as many special events as you can. I always tried to have something going on at least every four to six weeks. In case you haven't noticed, larger churches tend to have things happening regularly—which draws attention to your church. In the churches I've pastored, I've had families visit our church and tell me they came because they noticed things going on at the church. Again, always advertise all of your special events. Most TV, radio stations and newspapers offer free public service announcements or news releases. You can also advertise special events many places online.

When planning special events, don't have preachers only—diversify. Have different kinds or types of speakers, testimonies, musicians, music groups, and anything you can think of. Use your imagination—have regular brain storming sessions with your leaders. People are attracted by different things. Use various types of events to attract people. I like to use music because it attracts people who may not come hear a person speak. We used everything from quartets to Christian rock styles. One pastor I know, who had built a large church from nothing, once said, "We do some carnal things to get people in the church because people are carnal (he didn't mean sinful things). Once we get them we can work the carnality out of them."

The need to build relationships within the community is essential in order to facilitate the dropping of threshold of revival growth. It is imperative that a growing church build a stronger, spiritual, church community and move the new or struggling church over that revival threshold. If an organism is not growing it is dying. A growing membership must continually reach outward to sustain needed growth and expansion for the future. If we just look close in the Bible we can find examples of the strategies listed above. The above strategies should be in all churches today.

CHAPTER 8

EQUIPPING PASTORAL LEADERS FOR CHURCH PLANTING

As we focus on the enlistment and equipping of churches for the task of sponsoring activities for new church plants, it is crucial to consider the gifts and qualification of the church plant developer or pastor. According to (I Timothy 3: 1-17), "Bishops must not be a novice or inexperienced person least he fall in the snare of the devil" It is so important that the church developer be one of experience and spiritual wisdom.

In this focus on planting and sponsoring churches, the role of leadership, in particular pastoral leadership will be very crucial to the involvement of churches in sponsoring activities. It is the responsibility of the church planter or prospective pastor *to lead* and guide in a way to bring special results by going in advance; to direct on a course or in a direction; to serve as a channel for. The task of partnering in church planting is one which requires sound leadership within the sponsoring church.

In most cases, this role is personified at least in part by the pastor of the sponsoring church. However, successful partnership in church planting will require shared leadership in the church plant by way of a church planting team. The above definition alludes to several roles of leadership.

The first is the role of leading by example. The role of the pastor of a sponsoring church in church planting is crucial. While the pastor may not have the ability to participate in much of the implementation of the church planting strategy, there ought to be no one in the partnering church that is more passionate about the vision that God has given for Kingdom building through church planting. The exemplary passion of the pastor is often caught and reproduced in the church planting leadership team and the church body.

The second role of leadership identified is that of giving direction. As indicated above, shared leadership in the process of planting a church is critical. In their book *Spiritual Leadership*, Henry and Richard Blackaby describe the role of a spiritual leader in part as the responsibility to move people from where they are to where God wants them to be. It is entirely possible that anywhere from a dozen to several hundred believers will be involved in some manner in your church plant. Broad participation necessitates wise coordination.

The third role of leadership identified is that of serving as a channel within which activities can occur. Effective leadership sets and defines appropriate boundaries in which team members can operate. It will rest on the sponsor church pastor and the church planting leadership team to determine and communicate such boundaries with all who are enlisted to participate in any manner in the implementation of the church planting strategy. Such clarity will create an atmosphere in which called and gifted on mission believers and entities can serve the Lord in a positive and rewarding manner.

There is a principle illustrated throughout Scripture which is: God will always provide all of the resources necessary for obeying His call and His commands. It is entirely probable that God has already placed within your church the leaders needed for the church planting leadership team. These may be on mission believers that serve in key roles in your current ministry structure or potential leaders who are being developed. Whichever is the case, the leadership base of your existing church will be expanded as you begin to implement your church planting partnership.

The ultimate leader is Jesus. He always watched the activities of the Father in order to know what He wants to do and where He was to do it. His mission was to seek and to save the lost and to serve others. In so many ways, including leadership, He left us an example that we should follow in His footsteps. Let's pray that the Father will enable us to lead like Jesus, in particular in church planting activities.

Challenges of Leadership in Church Planting

Conflict in the ministry is a complex and challenging subject. It is an area that most who lead the church would prefer to avoid. However, anyone who has been in ministry for any length of time has experienced conflict. Someone once said that "conflict is neither good nor evil—but only inevitable".

Is it wrong to have differences of opinion in the church? Certainly not! Much of the conflict we encounter in the church is the result of change. Does this mean we avoid change altogether? No! But certain principles if followed will ensure successful change and a resolution to conflict.

A pastor should not treat his members with a "them or us attitude, if so, there will be trouble in the camp. Instead, a pastor needs to meet with the key leadership in the church and help them determine why their church exists. Until the pastor and church leaders can get on the same page concerning the mission of the church or church plant, there will be challenges at every turn in the road. We have to acknowledge the fact that there may be someone in the church plant group that may have a different vision of what God is trying to do. Ultimately, this difference of opinion may result in someone leaving the ministry. The separation must not hinder the direction God is leading but give more zeal to complete the vision and mission God has revealed.

Acts 2:42-47 clearly delineates the mission of the church. The pastor must teach and preach this purpose. It is wise not to talk about vision, and also avoid launching any ministry until you and your congregation have thoroughly come to terms with why your ministry exists, and have become people of worship, people who are biblically committed in relationship to one another, who are growing as disciples of Jesus Christ, and who are reaching the lost. In other words, having an understanding or shared vision, purpose and direction will tremendously add to the success of your ministry effort.

If we are going to be successful in ministry as pastors, developers or church planters, there is a need to meet with your team and determine if they understand why the church or ministry exists? Years ago while pasturing; I was surprised to hear the many different answers I received about the current ministry I was leading. At least your team which includes department heads, deacon, board members, and ministry leaders should know why Jesus established the church in the world. Only by experiencing shared vision can peace and agenda harmony exist within the church family.

When there are ten different answers to one question, there is a long road ahead in leading God's people to the next level. Only by using patience and godly wisdom can the ministry that God gives us can thrive and experience spiritual blessings. Instead of creating discord, open the scriptures and reason with the people from the word of God.

It is imperative that church planters find common ground and a base on which to build ministry. It is all about building relationship with the people God has given you to work with. It may take one year or even five years and sometimes never in leading followers where God wants them to be. If it takes a year to do this, don't do anything else until you get there. Once this common ground is understood, conflict will diminish in the church. In leading the church, the pastor-church planter needs to get everyone's agenda on the table. Remember, it's not what you want to do or what I want to do; it's what we should be during. The issue becomes focused on purpose. If reaching the lost is one of our reasons for being, then we need to decide how we are going to accomplish this. If my idea is not what you believe is right, then what is your idea? But we are going to reach the lost, because that's our mission.

I found a couple of principles that will assist pastors in guiding their congregation: understanding the mission of the church, and understanding the biblical philosophy of ministry in Ephesians 4 and how to implement this philosophy. Pastors should understand that the biblical philosophy of ministry is to equip God's people for works of service—for ministry. We've given lip service to that for years, but we must now implement it. As long as the pastor is the doer, and the people sit around determining how well the pastor does it, you have produced a system that creates conflict. People in the church will only find fulfillment when they are fulfilling the calling and the gifts of God in their lives. Only then will you have a church with happy people. Otherwise, they will be frustrated because they know they are not using what God has given them. But they don't know what to do about it, because we haven't taught them. It is important to take the opportunity to teach the people the direction God wants them to go.

When the pastor/church planter has gone through all the proper steps, and he still has someone who doesn't want to follow him or the vision God has given; How do you work with this person? If you have those in leadership who seem to be against everything you want to accomplish, ask that they help you understand why they are opposing you. Often you discover issues that have nothing to do with what they are opposing.

Over the past twenty six years of serving as pastor, I have encountered much opposition toward programs that I attempted to bring to the church body. When I begin to investigate why, I discovered circumstances that happened with another pastor, culture differences, and spiritual immaturity; as some of the major reasons for resistance. I learned after talking and working through the problem that often times it was not the recommendation but other personal thoughts and emotions that had to be brought out in the open. I believe by working with people and being willing to confront or discuss differences, the pastor or church planter can use the opportunity to build a lasting relationship.

There will be individuals who will never agree with the vision, no matter how simplistic the pastor or planter share the vision. At that point, it's the desire and will of the church that matters. Pastors need to fulfill God's purpose for their lives in and through the church. The church must seek to proceed, even when there are those who disagree.

I have never seen anything accomplished in my pastoral ministry that did not have people who said we couldn't do it, and it would never happen. But after it happened, they were ready to rejoice in all the good things God had done. Remember, Jesus lost one of the Twelve. Not everyone is going to follow the pastor's leadership. But it is important that pastors do everything they can, from their perspective, to encourage a person to follow. There are no accolades for pastors bragging about how many people have left the church. If you are a shepherd, you have a heart for God and for people. You will grieve over any loss. This doesn't mean you let people sabotage your ability to move forward; but love people and have a heart for them. It hurts when people oppose you or leaves the church. A good strategy is to attempt leading people where they want to go and avoid forcing them to where they don't want to go.

It is a grave error to force or browbeat people to follow you. Most memberships are turned off by autocratic styles of leadership. Pastors who don't understand this are going to have difficulty leading. I have found that people will commit to something that is going to make a difference in their lives, that will help them feel valued, and will help them fulfill the call of God in their lives. The ministry is not about the pastor; it's about people. The pastor's job as spiritual leader is to see that the people in the congregation succeed and growth in their spiritual walk.

To be effective, pastors need to be consistent in leadership. Over the years pastors have told people what they believed God had said to them, but their follow-through has been lacking. When this happens, pastors lose credibility and difficulties will eventually occur.

People who have been abused and hurt by authority bring that baggage to the church. People have a tendency to do one of two things with a spiritual leader: either not trusts anybody in spiritual leadership because they have been hurt; or, they will put the leader on a pedestal because the pastor represents the authority they never had in their lives. Both are equally dangerous for a pastor. If they put you on a pedestal, all you have to do is make one mistake in their eyes, and they will remove you from that pedestal so fast you will never know what hit you. The best thing you can do as a pastor is to make sure you operate with integrity. Follow through on the commitments you make, and love people. These qualities will help you gain respect with the congregants.

The Emotional Challenges of Ministry:

There are many secret emotions that insert themselves into the humanity of human leaders. Many times the church planter/developer keep these emotions inside and is very reluctant in sharing these inner feeling with others. Some of these emotions are as follows:

Self-Pity:

Self-pity is a result of two common habits: first, when we compare ourselves to others; and second, when we compete with others. When I start comparing or competing, I end up feeling discouraged because there are always those who are further along or better than I am in certain areas of life. 2 Cor. 10:12 ". . . and comparing themselves among themselves, are not wise." Surely, there isn't a profession more proficient at comparing and competing than pastors. Pray for them. That's the best cure for bitterness and unforgiveness. Taking the moral high ground to pray for your "competitors" keeps you in the place where God can minister to your heart. As a pastor, you must beware of comparing your church with others'. There will always be a church with a larger attendance, a larger sanctuary, a larger youth ministry, and a larger income. You may get discouraged if you hear that a pastor friend had a larger Easter crowd than you had, or if another church bought a bigger piece of land than you bought. You can't judge your own ministry by comparing it with another's. Seek the Lord for wisdom to know how you can produce fruit in God's Kingdom. Our purpose in ministry is to further the Gospel and build up the Body of Christ. Our purpose is not to beat out another church and be able to brag about our Easter attendance.

Fear of Failure and Failure Itself:

The fear of failure must be avoided if a Leader desires to experience growth in his or her personal and professional life. Ministers commonly face this fear, being apprehensive about making a mistake. "What if I make this move and discover that it wasn't God?" In my own thought life, I have learned to respond to this question by admitting that people have seen us do many things that didn't work. A pastor making a mistake periodically isn't going to surprise his people. Accept the fact that mistakes will be made; this will reduce a great deal of the fear that plagues your mind. After you make a mistake, just try again. "For a just man falleth seven times, and riseth up again" (Prov. 24:16). A primary reason why it is easy for our church to try new things is that I am not afraid to make a mistake. For example, we started a Saturday night service a few years ago. While the staff was casting the vision to the congregation, someone asked, "What if it doesn't work?" I answered, "Then we'll stop doing it." A similar situation occurred when we went to two services on Sunday morning. A church member wondered, "What if no one shows up to the early service?" I answered the same as before. I am not afraid to miss it in life or in ministry. I believe that change is a natural characteristic of leadership, and I accept the fact that mistakes go hand in hand with change. We can miss God as easily by doing nothing as we can by moving forward. The most effective leaders are willing to risk failure to achieve success. What risk do you need to take right now?

Fear of Rejection:

A fear of rejection begins to plague us when we seek to draw our security from the crowd. As long as we seek to draw our security from our people, we are unable to lead them into God's security. Many fear that if they are not acting like the rest of the crowd, they will be rejected. What crowds are you afraid might reject you? For some, that crowd is their congregation. For others, the crowd is their peers, while others fear rejection from businesspeople in the community. Some people avoid doing something out of the ordinary and rising above the status quo because they fear the rejection of others. We must realize that to be accepted by God means that people will sometimes reject us. There will be people who do not like you no matter how well you hear God's voice. Jesus is the prime example of this fact. Remember when the people tried to throw Jesus off a cliff after He proclaimed that the Spirit of the Lord was on Him? (Luke 4:29) Although He was doing God's will, people weren't satisfied. Rejection is a part of life. We cannot afford to let it ruin our life, or to keep us from stepping out in faith. Recall what Jesus said to Paul, that life-changing moment when Paul was converted on the road to Damascus: "(I am) Delivering thee from the people, and from the Gentiles, unto whom now I send thee" (Acts 26:17). God wants to deliver you and me from the people He's sent us to, so that we don't have to fear rejection from them. We can't be afraid that church members will leave, or that your staff will go start another church. These things can happen, but we can't live in fear. Address the fears you face. Identify those areas that cripple or paralyze you and tackle them. Start by honestly bringing these before the Lord in prayer. One of the best characteristics a person can develop to overcome fear is perspective. The ability to see people and issues in light of eternity will change your life. One million years from now as we worship the Lord, those issues we face today will have a slightly different value. Having the discipline to see what is around us with the perspective of eternity will give us confidence in the presence of fear.

Loneliness:

The job of a leader will be lonely at times. Leading means you are out ahead of the crowd—and that is a lonely position. All presidents have experienced the loneliness that accompanies their job. The day that the Gulf War began, President Bush walked the gardens at the White House for hours, agonizing over the fact that his decision would cause the deaths of many people. That day, he learned the loneliness of leadership. Abraham Lincoln, feeling the weight of leadership he carried alone, would get up in the middle of the night and walk the streets of Washington. When I teach at a conference, one of my main objectives is to help build relationships between the pastors. Ministers often feel that there is no one out there to talk to. When the pressure hits and they make decisions without adequate support, they sometimes find those decisions to be fatal to their ministry.

Simply building friendships with other pastors can alleviate some of the feelings of loneliness and the costly errors it can cause. I remember how desperate I was for the advice and encouragement from other, more established pastors when I started pastoring a small church out in west Texas. I reached out to another pastor for understanding and advice as to what could be done to save my rapidly failing church. "Don't you remember what it was like to be a small and struggling church?" I asked. "No, and I hope I never do," was his answer. His response is part of the reason I am so inspired to reach out to help young pastors today. If through my experiences I can help someone—if we as a group of pastors can encourage and teach others by our successes and failures, then the Body of Christ will be made stronger. Today let me encourage you that you are not alone, and that the difficult emotions so common to many leaders can be worked out by the grace of God. 1) 'Stress now contributes to 90% of all diseases. Half of all visits to doctors are stress-related'. 'Anxiety reduction' may now be the largest single business in the Western world. (2) 'Doctors, lawyers and clergy have the most problems with drug abuse, alcoholism and suicide.' (3) 'Research 25 years ago showed clergy dealing with stress better than most professionals. Since 1980, studies in the U.S. describe an alarming spread of burnout in the profession. For example, Jerdon found three out of four parish ministers (sample: 11,500) reported severe stress causing 'anguish, worry, bewilderment, anger, depression, fear, and alienation'.

Physical and Emotional Stress:

The reasons may be as numerous and unique as there are pastors. However, recent research is unanimous in citing the following problem areas: the disparity between (somewhat idealistic) expectations and hard reality; lack of clearly defined boundaries—tasks are never done; workaholism ('bed-at-the-church' syndrome); the Peter Principle—feeling of incompetence in leading an army of volunteers; conflict in being a leader and servant at the same time ('line-support contamination'); intangibility—how do I know I'm getting somewhere?; confusion of role identity with self image—pastors derive too much self-esteem from what they do; time management problems (yet pastors have more 'discretionary time' than any other professional group); paucity of 'perks'; multiplicity of roles; inability to produce 'win-win' conflict resolutions; difficulty in managing interruptions; the 'little adult' syndrome (Dittes)—clergy are too serious, they have difficulty being spontaneous; preoccupation with 'playing it safe' to avoid enraging powerful parishioners; 'administration overload'—too much energy expended in areas of low reward; loneliness—the pastor is less likely to have a close friend than any other person in the community. STRESS Stress and burn out are not the same (see box). Hans Selye defines stress in terms of the response your body makes to any demand on it. There is 'good stress' (eustress)—associated with feelings of joy, fulfillment, achievement—and 'bad stress' (distress), which is prolonged or too-frequent stress. It is not possible (without a frontal lobotomy) to live without stress. Originally the term came from physics: the application of sufficient force to an object to distort it. So stress comes from 'outside' the organism, causing your body to respond in either 'fight' (when angry) or 'flight' (fear). Actually, stress is the transaction that takes place between you and your environment. The outside event impinges on your belief system, your brain interprets what's happening, and tells your body how to respond. Adrenalin is pumped into your bloodstream; blood is diverted from various organs to brain and muscles; pupils dilate (making vision more acute); hands and feet perspire; breathing and heart-rate increase, etc. The body is on 'red alert', the alarm response. Most of us are not subject to physical danger very often, but whenever you are 'driven' by a very tight program, or threatened by a demand or expectation you don't think you can meet, your body reacts in the same way. In fact, medical experts are now saying that 'Type A' people in particular may be suffering a kind of 'adrenalin addiction'. Dr. David McClelland, professor of psychology at Harvard, says stress addiction is similar to the state of physiological arousal some people derive from a dependency on alcohol, caffeine and nicotine. A recent book Management and the Brain (Soujanen and Bessinger) suggest that some professionals are actually 'hooked' on stress. They get a 'high' out of controlling people and making complex decisions. Dr. Paul Rosch, president of the American Institute of Stress, says the Type A male (50% of all pastors are Type A, according to Dr. Arch Hart) who is 'living in the fast lane . . . has become addicted to his own adrenalin and unconsciously seeks ways to get those little surges'. These days more of us will die from a stress-related illness than from infection or old age. The only advantage of living stressfully: you'll get to meet your Lord earlier!

Burn Out:

Burnout is emotional exhaustion, *'compassion fatigue'*. All Christians can and will off suffer burnout. The most conscientious people-helpers are most vulnerable. Researchers like Maslach, Freudenberger and others from 1977 onwards gave the name *'burn-out'* to the special stressors associated with social and interpersonal pressures. Dr. Arch Hart says burnout symptoms may include demoralization (belief you are not longer effective as a pastor); depersonalization (treating yourself and others in an impersonal way); detachment (withdrawing from responsibilities); distancing (avoidance of social and interpersonal contacts); and defeatism (a feeling of being 'beaten'). Christina Maslach, who described burnout as 'a state of physical, emotional and mental exhaustion marked by physical depletion and chronic fatigue, feelings of helplessness and hopelessness, and by development of a negative self-concept and negative attitudes towards work, life and other people', offers the following signs: (1) Decreased energy—*'keeping up the speed'* becomes increasingly difficult; (2) feeling of failure in vocation; (3) reduced sense of reward in return for pouring so much of self into the job or project; (4) a sense of helplessness and inability to see a way out of problems; and (5) cynicism and negativism about self, others, work and the world generally. Personality and attitudinal factors may increase the propensity to burnout eg.: the pressure to succeed; an authoritarian personality which may come across insensitively (or a too-sensitive person who can feel with others' hurts but who is vulnerable to criticism); inner-directed rage; under assertiveness—feeling victimized; carrying too much guilt about our humanness (an occupational hazard for clergy, so we develop facades for various occasions); inflexibility; and many more. The essence of the problem, however, is the clash between expectations and reality. Clergy are often put on a pedestal—by others, and by themselves. Many of these expectations just can't be met. We try to please, but may either become too goal-oriented for our people, or else too accommodating to their spiritual 'slackness'.

'Strongly goal-oriented ministers will almost inevitably experience more frustration than process-oriented ones'. This why totally surrendering to God is the best way to combat emotional distress in ministry.

Equipping Oneself for Spiritual Warfare:

The difference between deliverance and spiritual warfare is that deliverance is dealing with demonic bondages, and getting a person set free, whereas spiritual warfare is resisting, overcoming and defeating the enemy's lies (in the form of deception, temptations and accusations) that he sends our way. Deliverance involves the breaking up of legal grounds, the tearing down of strongholds (offensive spiritual warfare), and the casting out of demons. Spiritual warfare on the other hand, is dealing with three key things the enemy sends at us: temptations, deception and accusations.

This teaching will give you an idea of how spiritual warfare works. There are other teachings on this site that will go into more detail on certain areas of spiritual warfare.

Offensive vs. defensive warfare:

Spiritual warfare comes in two ways: offensive and defensive. Offensive warfare is tearing down the strongholds the enemy has formed in your mind through deception and accusations, and defensive warfare is guarding yourself against the tactics or schemes of the devil.

The enemy's three primary weapons:

There are three things that we can expect from the devil. The Bible tells us that we struggle not against flesh and blood, but against demonic forces. Ephesians 6:12, "For we wrestle not against flesh and blood, but against principalities, against powers, against the rulers of the darkness of this world, against spiritual wickedness in high places." The three primary things we struggle against include:

#1 Deception: To deceive somebody means to make another person believe a lie or something that is not true. When the enemy sends deception our way, it is an attempt to deceive you into believing something that is not true, so you will fall into error. Strongholds are built through deception. A stronghold is formed when deception takes hold in a person's mind. A stronghold is an incorrect thinking pattern that stems from believing something that is not true.

From the very beginning, Satan deceived Eve into believing that God's Word was not true. In Genesis 3:4, the devil told her that she will not surely die as God said she would in Genesis 2:17.

#2 Temptations: Temptation often follows deception. First the enemy tells us, "You won't surely die!", and then he makes the fruit on the forbidden tree look good to us. Since Eve accepted Satan's deception (his lie), now the tree that she was not supposed to touch looked good to her. She was tempted (enticed) to sin, because she allowed herself to first be deceived. Temptation is when we are enticed or encouraged to sin in one way or another.

In Matthew 4, Jesus was led out in the desert to be tempted by the devil. The devil tried to convince Jesus that it would be harmless to jump off a building. Often people will be so drawn to sex with their boyfriend/girlfriend when the enemy tries to convince them that it is all harmless and fun, when it's not harmless at all, but an open door to the devil. Jesus saw through Satan's deception, and resisted the temptation by speaking God's Word. King David said in Psalms 119:11, "Thy word have I hid in mine heart, that I might not sin against thee."

When the enemy tempts you, he's showing you the worm . . . but behind that worm is a hook. The Word of God helps you see the hook behind the worm.

#3 Accusations: The devil is known as the accuser of the brethren (Rev 12:10). He is known to take a believer who has done an embarrassing or gross sin in their past, and continue to rub it in their faces and beat them down with guilt and condemnation over their past.

Dealing with Deception:

We have two weapons to deal with deceptions: the belt of truth (Ephesians 6:14) and the sword of the Spirit (Ephesians 6:17) which is the Word of God. Both are truth, which is found in God's Word, so why are they given two different names (a sword and a belt)? The word of God has two ingredients, one is meant to be defensive (the belt), while the other is meant to be offensive (the sword). This means that the Word of God is both an offensive and a defensive weapon. A belt is something you wear to guard against an attack, while a sword is used to slaughter the enemy. You use the belt of truth (God's Word) to guard against the enemy's deception (lies) he sends your way, while you use the sword of the Spirit (also God's Word) to tear down existing strongholds (deception that took hold) in your mind.

In Romans 12:2, we are told to "be not conformed to this world: but are ye transformed by the renewing of your mind." How do we renew our minds? By getting in God's Word! In Ephesians 5:26, this process is referred to as washing of water by the Word: "That he might sanctify and cleanse it with the washing of water by the word."

Dealing with Temptation:

In James 4:7, we are told to resist the devil and he will flee from us. But it's not that simple; in the same verse, we are also told to draw near to God. Dealing with temptation is a twofold process of resisting the devil and drawing near to God. The closer you get to God and the more we become aware of His love, the less power temptation will have over you. James 4:7, "Submit yourselves therefore to God; Resist the devil, and he will flee from you."

Dealing with Accusations:

The fiery darts of the enemy in Ephesians 6:16 are accusations sent our way. For example, when the devil tries to accuse us of our past sins, we are to have faith in the work of the cross and know that they are forgiven and not to look back. Faith is what we use to put out the fiery darts of the enemy (Ephesians 6:16). We are not to meditate about our pasts, because they have passed away (2 Corinthians 5:17), and our sins have been forgotten (Hebrews 10:17). Ephesians 6:14, "Stand therefore, having your loins girt about with truth (knowing your sins have been forgiven through your faith in the work on the cross), and having on the breastplate of righteousness (not our righteousness obviously, but the righteousness of God through Christ Jesus);"

Our righteousness is as filthy rags (Isaiah 64:6), but because of the work of the cross, we can receive the righteousness of God through Christ Jesus (Romans 3:22, Galatians 3:6). Therefore when the enemy tries to remind you of your past, tell him it's been washed away (2 Corinthians 5:17), your sins have been forgotten (Hebrews 10:17) and you have the righteousness of God (Romans 3:22)!

There are other teachings on this site that will specifically help you wage war against the enemy's accusations

The tearing down of Strongholds:

A stronghold is deception that's taken hold in a person's mind. It's an incorrect thinking pattern based on a believed lie. People can get incorrect perceptions of God by listening to Satan as he tells them how God doesn't love them, etc. People can feel like dirty old sinners when they believe Satan's accusations as he continually reminds them of their past (which has been washed away!). Strongholds are based on lies from the devil. They can come in the form of deception or accusations. Accusations always lead to guilt and the feeling of unworthiness, which weighs you down and tears you apart spiritually.

Since strongholds are built upon lies that we have been fed, the way we tear down strongholds is by feeding on the truth (in God's Word), which is the opposite of what the enemy has been feeding us. If the enemy has been feeding us a lie, we need to stop eating the lie and start feeding ourselves the truth. The weapon we use to tear down strongholds is found in Ephesians 6:17, ". . . the sword of the Spirit, which is the word of God." A sword is an offensive weapon and is meant to tear down and kill the enemy's troops. Strongholds are the devil's assets in war, and he uses them against us. Take up the sword of the Spirit (God's Word) today, and start slaughtering the enemy's assets that he's been using against you! Only then can you obtain the victory God has given you through His son Jesus Christ.

SUMMARY AND CONCLUSION

In looking back through the recorded history of God's work in Scripture, you will see that God used ordinary people—even the most unlikely of people—to change the world and accomplish His will. God used a young shepherd boy named David. He used Abraham, Moses, Rahab, Esther, and Mary and Joseph. Even the Apostles were ordinary individuals used by God to do extraordinary things. These were people called by God for His glory; His honor. Although every Christian is called to serve the cause of Christ, God calls certain persons to serve the church as pastors, evangelists, teachers, and other ministers, and some as church planters.

Shortly after His baptism, Jesus dwelt by the Sea of Galilee. It was here that He called His first disciples—Peter and Andrew, James and John—all ordinary folks; fishermen who were used by God to change the course of history. God is calling us in our present field to be a witness for him. The disciples were hard working, salt-of-the-earth kind of people. They were used, called by God, for His glory. God wants to use each of us where we are to accomplish His will.

Take another look at the calling of the disciples. First, they were called to a person, to Christ Himself. He said they were to follow Him. Second, they were called for a purpose. He was going to make them fishers of men.

They left the security of their homes, their families, and their occupations to follow Jesus. Thirdly, God often calls us to an uncomfortable place. A place it appears that is far from friends and family—a calling to a place unknown, but certainly not close to home.

In church planting, God calls us to deny ourselves, to take up our crosses and follow Him. We understand that it is all about priorities, about who rules our lives. There are those who marvel about the commitment made to sacrifice to receive heavenly rewards. They marvel at our faith, our spirituality.

Those of us who have been called by God to forsake everything: family, friends and occupations, are called neither clergy and or God's servants. A very popular story came to my mind in the eighth chapter of Matthew. The Bible says, as Jesus is entering into Capernaum, a Roman soldier approaches Him. He is distraught. One of his servants is deathly sick. Jesus sees his anguish. He has compassion and offers to travel with him to his home. The man, aware of Jewish customs, tells Jesus no. A Jew cannot enter into the home of a Gentile without being defiled. He tells Jesus he is unworthy of His presence but asks Jesus to speak a word of healing, to command the illness to depart from his servant.

Jesus "marveled" at the man's faith. He even declares, "I have not found such great faith, not even in Israel!" I want you to see something that you may have not seen before. Look at what Jesus says to the man, "Go your way . . . ." Now take a look at what He didn't say. Remember this man's faith? Why didn't Jesus say to this man, "Come, and follow me?" Why didn't Jesus command this man to forsake family, friends and his occupation? After all, he is a Roman soldier. Shouldn't he be commanded to follow Christ, to leave everything behind? Why didn't Jesus command the man to follow Him? Why didn't Jesus ask the man to leave behind his career, family and friends? Because we are all called by God for a purpose, but few are called to another place. Most are called to where they are, to live out and proclaim the gospel of Jesus right where they are. His calling was to be expressed in his present vocation. Think about it . . . he was called by God to be a missionary in the midst of the Roman army! So are we in our current locations.

We can impact the lives of those who we see each day with the hope of the Gospel. All this can take place in the community in which we live.

If we are going to reach our communities with the gospel, we must consider the new church plant process. There is a need for experienced pastors or church developers who will be willing to take a walk of faith. Religious organizations will need hundreds of new church planters to develop churches among diverse groups. Men and women called to a person . . . for a purpose . . . and to a place . . . in the workplace, in our neighborhoods, amongst our peers and families. We are going to have to rethink our strategy and return to a place where ordinary, everyday Christ-followers assume the bulk of the work. We are going to have to remove the barrier between clergy and laity and engage every day, ordinary service laborers in the field of harvest. Church planters are called to leave all to follow Christ. The greatest work any Christian believer can do is to involve themselves by making a difference in the community in which they live. It is my desire that this written ready reference handbook will be a focal point and blessing to those who feel God's call to explore the church planting experience.

COPYRIGHT ACKNOWLEDGEMENTS

Bennett, Shane, Kim Felder and Steve Hawthorne. (1995) *Exploring the Land*. Littleton, Colo.: Caleb Project

Blackaby, Henry T. and Richard. (2001) *Spiritual Leadership: Moving People on to God* Nashville, TN;

Tom, and Warren Bird. (2001) *Lost in America: How You and Your Church Can Impact the World Next Door*. Loveland, Colo.: Group Publishing

William P. Dillon. (1993) *People Raising: A Practical Guide to Raising Support*. Chicago: Moody Press

Hybels, B. (2002) (McArthur Jr, John. *Learning How to Develop Shared Ministry Values*.

Courageous Leadership. Grand Rapids: Zondervan Publishers

Miller, G. (2005) The Calling. The Realities of the Gospel Ministry: Pleasant Word: Wine Press Publishing

Robb, John D. Focus! (1994) *The Power of People Group Thinking*. Monrovia, Calif.: MARC Publications

Stanley, A. (1999) *Visioneering*. Sistera, Ore.: Multnomah Publishers

Wagner, P. (1996) Possessing The Gates Of The Enemy. Grand Rapids Warren. R. (1995) *The Purpose-Driven Church*. Grand Rapids:

Zondervan

www.ingramcontent.com/pod-product-compliance
Lightning Source LLC
LaVergne TN
LVHW092052060526
838201LV00047B/1362